Quantum Computing and
Other Transformative Technologies

RIVER PUBLISHERS SERIES IN COMPUTING AND INFORMATION SCIENCE AND TECHNOLOGY

Series Editors

K.C. CHEN
National Taiwan University,
Taipei, Taiwan

University of South Florida,
USA

SANDEEP SHUKLA
Virginia Tech,
USA

Indian Institute of Technology Kanpur,
India

The "River Publishers Series in Computing and Information Science and Technology" covers research which ushers the 21st Century into an Internet and multimedia era. Networking suggests transportation of such multimedia contents among nodes in communication and/or computer networks, to facilitate the ultimate Internet.

Theory, technologies, protocols and standards, applications/services, practice and implementation of wired/wireless

The "River Publishers Series in Computing and Information Science and Technology" covers research which ushers the 21st Century into an Internet and multimedia era. Networking suggests transportation of such multimedia contents among nodes in communication and/or computer networks, to facilitate the ultimate Internet.

Theory, technologies, protocols and standards, applications/services, practice and implementation of wired/wireless networking are all within the scope of this series. Based on network and communication science, we further extend the scope for 21st Century life through the knowledge in machine learning, embedded systems, cognitive science, pattern recognition, quantum/biological/ molecular computation and information processing, user behaviors and interface, and applications across healthcare and society.

Books published in the series include research monographs, edited volumes, handbooks and textbooks. The books provide professionals, researchers, educators, and advanced students in the field with an invaluable insight into the latest research and developments.

Topics included in the series are as follows:-

- Artificial Intelligence
- Cognitive Science and Brian Science
- Communication/Computer Networking Technologies and Applications
- Computation and Information Processing
- Computer Architectures
- Computer Networks
- Computer Science
- Embedded Systems
- Evolutionary Computation
- Information Modelling
- Information Theory
- Machine Intelligence
- Neural Computing and Machine Learning
- Parallel and Distributed Systems
- Programming Languages
- Reconfigurable Computing
- Research Informatics
- Soft Computing Techniques
- Software Development
- Software Engineering
- Software Maintenance

For a list of other books in this series, visit www.riverpublishers.com

Quantum Computing and Other Transformative Technologies

Ahmed Banafa

Professor of Engineering at San Jose State University (USA)
and
Instructor of Continuing Studies at Stanford University (USA)

NEW YORK AND LONDON

Published 2023 by River Publishers

River Publishers

Alsbjergvej 10, 9260 Gistrup, Denmark

www.riverpublishers.com

Distributed exclusively by Routledge

605 Third Avenue, New York, NY 10017, USA

4 Park Square, Milton Park, Abingdon, Oxon OX14 4RN

Quantum Computing and Other Transformative Technologies / Ahmed Banafa.

Routledge is an imprint of the Taylor & Francis Group, an informa business

ISBN 978-87-7022-684-4 (print)

ISBN 978-10-0079-432-8 (online)

ISBN 978-1-003-33917-5 (ebook master)

While every effort is made to provide dependable information, the publisher, authors, and editors cannot be held responsible for any errors or omissions.

Dedication

In the loving memory of my son Malik

Contents

Preface   xvii

Audience   xix

Acknowledgment   xxi

List of Figures   xxiii

List of Abbreviations   xxv

Introduction   1

Part 1   Quantum Computing   3
1 What is Quantum Computing?   5
   1.1   A Comparison of Classical and Quantum Computing   5
   1.2   Quantum Superposition and Entanglement   6
   1.3   Difficulties with Quantum Computers   6
   1.4   The Future of Quantum Computing.   7
   References.   7

2 Quantum Cryptography   9
   2.1   Problems with using Quantum Cryptography.   10
   References.   11

3 Quantum Internet   13
   3.1   What is Quantum Internet?   14
   3.2   Quantum Communications   15
   References.   16

4 Quantum Teleportation   17
   4.1   Quantum Teleportation: Paving the Way for a
          Quantum Internet   19
   References.   19

5 Quantum Computing and IoT   **21**
  5.1   A Comparison of Classical and Quantum Computing   22
  5.2   Quantum Communications   23
  5.3   Quantum Computing and IoT   24
  5.4   The Road Ahead   24
  References   25

6 Quantum Computing and Blockchain: Myths and Facts   **27**
  6.1   Difficulties with Quantum Computers   27
  6.2   What Is Quantum Supremacy?   28
  6.3   What is Quantum Cryptography?   29
  References   30

7 Quantum Computing and AI: A Mega-Buzzword   **31**
  7.1   What is Quantum Computing?   31
  7.2   Difficulties with Quantum Computers   32
  7.3   Applications of Quantum Computing and AI   32
  7.4   Processing Large Sets of Data   32
  7.5   Solve Complex Problem Faster   33
  7.6   Better Business Insights and Models   33
  7.7   Integration of Multiple Sets of Data   34
  7.8   The Future   34
  References   34

8 Quantum Computing Trends   **37**
  8.1   A Comparison of Classical and Quantum Computing   37
  8.2   Physical vs. Logical Qubits   38
  8.3   Quantum Superposition and Entanglement   39
  8.4   Quantum Emulator/Simulator   40
  8.5   Quantum Annealer   40
  8.6   Noisy Intermediate-Scale Quantum (NISQ) Computers . . .   40
  8.7   Universal Quantum Computers/Cryptographically Relevant
        Quantum Computers (CRQC)   41
  8.8   Post-Quantum/Quantum-Resistant Codes   41
  8.9   Difficulties with Quantum Computers   41
  References   41

Part 2   Other Computing Technologies   **43**
9 What is Deep Learning?   **45**
  9.1   Neural Network   45
  9.2   Deep Learning vs. Machine Learning   46

9.3   The Deep Learning Game   46
9.4   The Future   47
References   47

10 Affective Computing   **49**
10.1   Emotion in Machines   50
10.2   The Future   51
References   51

11 Autonomic Computing   **53**
11.1   Benefits   55
11.2   Future of Autonomic Computing   55
References   55

Part 3   Big Data, Dark Data, Thick Data, and Small Data   **57**
12 Thick Data vs. Big Data   **59**
12.1   Comparison of Big Data and Thick Data   60
References   62

13 Understanding Dark Data   **65**
13.1   Types of Dark Data   66
13.2   Value of Dark Data   66
13.3   Future of Dark Data   67
References   67

14 Small Data vs. Big Data: Back to the Basics   **69**
14.1   Why Small Data?   70
14.2   The Future of Small Data   71
References   72

15 What is a Data Lake?   **73**
15.1   Data Lake vs. Data Warehouse   73
15.2   Five Key Components of a Data Lake Architecture   74
15.3   Data Lake Advantages   75
15.4   Data Lake Disadvantages   76
15.5   The Future   76
References   77

Part 4   Cloud Computing   **79**
16 Edge Computing Paradigm   **81**
16.1   Advantages of Edge Computing   82
16.2   Benefits of Edge Computing   83

16.3   Real-Life Example   83
16.4   Future of Edge Computing   84
References   85

17 The Internet of Everything   **87**
17.1   What is the Internet of Everything (IoE)?   87
17.2   Pillars of the Internet of Everything (IoE)   88
17.3   The Internet of Things (IoT)   88
17.4   The Difference Between IoE and IoT   88
17.5   The Future   88
References   89

18 Content Delivery Networks – CDNs   **91**
18.1   Dynamics of CDNs.   91
18.2   Difference Between Serving Content without a CDN and
       with a CDN.   92
18.3   Types of Services.   94
18.4   Advantages of CDNs.   94
18.5   Disadvantages of CDNs   95
18.6   The Future   95
References   95

19 Network Functions Virtualization (NFV) or Software-Defined
Networking (SDN)?   **97**
19.1   What is Network Functions Virtualization (NFV)?   97
19.2   The Benefits of NFV   98
19.3   Types of NFV   98
19.4   Which is Better – SDN or NFV?.   99
19.5   The Future of NFV   100
References   100

20 What is Virtualization?   **101**
20.1   What is Virtualization?.   101
20.2   Types of Virtualizations   102
20.3   How is Virtualization Different from Cloud Computing? . .   103
20.4   The Future of Virtualization   103
References   103

21 Risks of Cloud Computing Explained (Both Sides)   **105**
21.1   The Risks Will Never Diminish   107
References   108

22 Cloud-of-Clouds or (Intercloud) **109**
   22.1   The Future 110
   References 111

23 Myths and Facts About Cloud Computing **113**
   23.1   Types of Cloud Computing. 113
   23.2   The Promise of Cloud Computing 115
   23.3   What is Next for Cloud Computing?. 116

Part 5   Security **119**

24 Zero-Day Vulnerability and Heuristic Analysis **121**
   24.1   What is a Zero-Day Vulnerability?. 121
   24.2   Zero-Day Exploit. 122
   24.3   Zero-Day Threat 122
   24.4   Defending Against Zero-Day Threats 122
   24.5   What are Heuristics? 123
   References 125

25 The Zero Trust Model **127**
   25.1   "Outside-In" to "Inside-Out" Attacks 128
   25.2   Zero Trust Recommendations 129
   References   129

26 Cloud Computing Security **131**
   26.1   Cloud Security Threats 132
   26.2   The Future 133

27 First Line of Defense for Cybersecurity: AI **135**
   27.1   Four Fundamental Security Practices 137
         27.1.1   Identifying the patterns 137
         27.1.2   Educating the users 137
         27.1.3   Patching the holes. 138
         27.1.4   Checking off the controls 138
   27.2   Challenges Faced by AI in Cybersecurity 138
         27.2.1   AI-powered attacks 138
         27.2.2   More sandbox-evading malware 139
         27.2.3   Ransomware and IoT 139
         27.2.4   A rise of state-sponsored attacks 140
         27.2.5   Shortage of skilled staff. 140
         27.2.6   IT infrastructure 140

27.3   The Future of Cybersecurity and AI   140
References   141

28 Second Line of Defense for Cybersecurity: Blockchain   **143**
28.1   Implementing Blockchain in Cybersecurity   144
28.2   Advantages of using Blockchain in Cybersecurity   145
    28.2.1   Decentralization   145
    28.2.2   Tracking and tracing   146
    28.2.3   Confidentiality   146
    28.2.4   Fraud security   146
    28.2.5   Sustainability   146
    28.2.6   Integrity   146
    28.2.7   Resilience   146
    28.2.8   Data quality   146
    28.2.9   Smart contracts   147
    28.2.10   Availability   147
    28.2.11   Increased customer trust   147
28.3   Disadvantages of using Blockchain in Cybersecurity   147
    28.3.1   Irreversibility   147
    28.3.2   Storage limits   147
    28.3.3   Risk of cyberattacks   147
    28.3.4   Adaptability challenges   148
    28.3.5   High operation costs   148
    28.3.6   Blockchain literacy   148
28.4   Conclusion   148
References   149

29 Network Security Needs Big Data   **151**
29.1   Zero Trust Model (ZTM)   152
29.2   Big Data and ZTM   153

Part 6   Blockchain   **155**
30 Blockchain Technology and COVID-19   **157**
30.1   Major Challenges of COVID-19   158
30.2   Can Blockchain Help in Preventing Pandemics?   158
30.3   Tracking Infectious Disease Outbreaks   159
30.4   Donations Tracking   159
30.5   Crisis Management   160
30.6   Securing Medical Supply Chains   160
30.7   WHO and Blockchain Technology   160
References   161

31 How Blockchain is Revolutionizing Crowdfunding   **163**
   31.1   Limitations of Current Crowdfunding Platforms 163
   31.2   How Blockchain Helps Crowdfunding 165
   References 166

32 Blockchain Technology and Supply Chain Management   **167**
   32.1   Blockchain and SCM. 168
   32.2   Applications of Blockchain in SCM 169
   References 169

Part 7   IoT   **171**
33 IoT and COVID-19   **173**
   33.1   IoT and WFH. 174
   33.2   IoT and Blockchain 174
   33.3   IoT and E-Commerce 175
   33.4   IoT and Telemedicine 175
   References 176

34 IoT and 5G Convergence   **177**
   34.1 Benefits of using 5G in IoT 178
         34.1.1   Higher transmission speed 178
         34.1.2   More devices connected 178
         34.1.3   Lower latency 179
   34.2   Challenges Faced by 5G and IoT Convergence 179
         34.2.1   Operating across multiple spectrum bands 179
         34.2.2   A gradual upgradation from 4G to 5G 179
         34.2.3   Data interoperability 180
         34.2.4   Establishing 5G business models 180
   34.3   Examples of Applications of 5G in IoT 180
         34.3.1   Automotive 180
         34.3.2   Industrial 181
         34.3.3   Healthcare. 181
   References 181

Part 8   Wearable and Mobile Technology   **183**
35 The Smart Platform: Wearable Computing Devices (WCD)   **185**
   35.1   Concerns with Wearable Computing Devices 186
   35.2   Applications of Wearable Computing Devices 186
   35.3   The Future of Wearable Computing Devices. 186
   References 187

36 Your Smart Device Will Feel Your Pain and Fear   **189**
References 192

37 Technology Under Your Skin: Three Challenges of Microchip
   Implants   **193**
References 196

Part 9   Future Trends in Technology   **197**
38 The Metaverse: A Different Perspective   **199**
   38.1   Different Perspective of the Metaverse 200
   38.2   Pillars of the Metaverse 200
   38.3   The Future 200
   References 201

39 The Metaverse: Myths and Facts   **203**
   39.1   Myths about the Metaverse. 204
        39.1.1   Myth #1: No one knows what the metaverse is. . . 204
        39.1.2   Myth #2: The metaverse is only gaming 204
        39.1.3   Myth #3: The metaverse is only virtual reality . . 204
        39.1.4   Myth #4: The metaverse will replace the
                 real world 204
        39.1.5   Myth #5: The metaverse is a fad 205
        39.1.6   Myth #6: The metaverse will be a monopoly . . . 205
        39.1.7   Myth #7: The speed of technology will set the
                 pace for adoption 206
        39.1.8   Myth #8: The metaverse is already here 206
        39.1.9   Myth #9: The metaverse is inevitable. 206
        39.1.10 Myth #10: The metaverse is suitable for
                 everything 207
   39.2   What is the Future of the Metaverse? 207
   References 208

40 Eight Key Tech Trends in a Post-COVID-19 World   **209**
   40.1   Artificial Intelligence (AI) 210
   40.2   Cloud Computing 211
   40.3   VR/AR 211
   40.4   5G Networks 211
   40.5   Voice User Interface (VUI). 212
   40.6   Internet of Things (IoT) 212
   40.7   Cybersecurity. 213

40.8   Blockchain Technology   213
40.9   Tracking Infectious Disease Outbreaks   214
40.10   Donations Tracking.   214
40.11   Crisis Management   215
40.12   Securing Medical Supply Chains   215
References   215

References   **217**

Index   **227**

About the Author   **231**

Preface

Quantum Computing is the area of study focused on developing computer technology based on the principles of quantum theory. Tens of billions of public and private capitals are being invested in quantum technologies. Countries across the world have realized that quantum technologies can be a major disruptor of existing businesses, they have collectively invested billions of dollars in quantum research and applications. In this book you will learn the difference between Quantum Computing and Classic Computing, also different categories of quantum computing will be discussed in details, applications of Quantum Computing in AI, IoT, Blockchain, Communications, and Encryption will be covered, in addition, Quantum Internet, Quantum Cryptography, Quantum Teleportation, and post-Quantum technologies will be explained. The book also covers other transformative technologies and their applications, advantages, and challenges, including; Affective Computing, Autonomic Computing, Big Data, Dark Data, Thick Data, and Small Data, along with Internet of Things (IoT), Blockchain, Cryptocurrency, Deep Learning, Cloud Computing, Edge/Fog Computing, 5G, and the Metaverse will be discussed. The important challenge of security in the world Quantum and non-Quantum Computing will be explained.

This book is divided into 9 parts:

Part 1 Quantum Computing
Part 2 Other Computing Technologies
Part 3 Big Data, Dark Data, Thick Data, and Small Data
Part 4 Cloud Computing
Part 5 Security
Part 6 Blockchain
Part 7 IoT
Part 8 Wearable and Mobile Technology
Part 9 Future Trends in Technology

Audience

This is book is for everyone who would like to have a good understanding of Quantum Computing and its applications and its relationship with business operations, and also gain insight to other transformative technologies like IoT, Cloud Computing, Deep Learning, Blockchain, Big Data and Wearable Technologies. Audience includes:

C-Suite executives, IT managers, marketing & sales professionals, lawyers, product & project managers, business professionals, journalists, students.

Acknowledgment

I am grateful for all the support I received from my family during the stages of writing this book.

List of Figures

Figure 4.1	Quantum entanglement..	18
Figure 7.1	Applications of quantum computing and AI.	33
Figure 8.1	Future of computing.	38
Figure 8.2	Quantum computuers categories.	39
Figure 12.1	Big data vs. Thick data.	61
Figure 15.1	Five key components of a data lake.	74
Figure 16.1	Edge computing.	82
Figure 16.2	Benefits of edge computing.	83
Figure 18.1	CDN types of services.	93
Figure 24.1	Defending against zero-day threats.	122
Figure 25.1	The zero-trust model three key concepts..	128
Figure 27.1	Four fundamental security practices.	136
Figure 27.2	Challenges faced using AI in cybersecurity.	138
Figure 28.1	Advantages of using blockchain in cybersecurity.	145
Figure 28.2	Disadvantages of using blockchain in cybersecurity..	147
Figure 30.1	What is COVID-19?	158
Figure 30.2	Blockchain applications in fighting COVID-19.	159
Figure 31.1	Limitations of current crowdfunding platforms.	164
Figure 31.2	Blockchain and crowdfunding.	165
Figure 32.1	Blockchain technology and supply chain management.	168
Figure 33.1	IoT and COVID-19..	174
Figure 34.1	Components of IoT.	178
Figure 37.1	Challenges facing microchip implant technology.	195
Figure 38.1	Components of the metaverse.	200
Figure 39.1	Seven layers of the metaverse.	205
Figure 40.1	Eight key tech trends in a post-COVID-19 world.	210
Figure 40.2	Blockchain applications in fighting COVID-19.	214

List of Abbreviations

ACI	Autonomic computing initiative
AI	Artificial intelligence
API	Application programming interface
AR	Augmented reality
AV	Antivirus
CAGR	Compound annual growth rate
CCPA	California consumer privacy act
CDN	Content delivery network
CIS	Center for Internet Security
CNSA	Commercial national security algorithm
CRM	Customer relationship management
CRQC	Cryptographically relevant quantum computer
CRQC	Cryptographically relevant quantum computers
DDoS	Distributed denial-of-service
DLT	Distributed ledger technology
DNS	Domain name service
DoE	Department of Energy
ECDSA	Elliptic curve digital signature algorithm
EM	Electromagnetic
ERP	Enterprise resource planning
GDRP	General data protection regulations
HIPAA	Health insurance portability and accountability act
HR	Human resources
ICO	Initial coin offering
IDC	International data corporation
IDS	Intrusion detection system
IIoT	Industrial Internet of Things
IoE	Internet of Everything
IoMT	Internet of Medical Things
IoT	Internet of Things

IP	Internet protocol
IPS	Intrusion prevention system
LPA	Least privilege access
MaaS	Metaverse as a service
ML	Machine learning
MLP	Machine learning poisoning
NAT	Network address translation
NFV	Network functions virtualization
NFV	Network functions virtualization
NISQ	Noisy intermediate scale quantum
NSA	National security agency
PaaS	Platforms-as-a-service
PAN	Personal area network
PCI	Payment card industry
QAI	Quantum artificial intelligence
QCaaS	Quantum computing as a service
QIaaS	Quantum infrastructure as a service
QIoT	Quantum IoT
QoS	Quality of service
QPaaS	Quantum platform as a service
QSaaS	Quantum software as a service
RFID	Radio-frequency identification
ROI	Return on investment
RSA	Rivest, Shamir, Adelman
SAN	Storage area network
SCM	Supply chain management
SDN	Software-defined networking
SEO	Search engine optimization
SNCA	Sensors, networks, cloud, and applications
SOX	Sarbanes-oxley act
SSL	Secure sockets layer
SSP	Safety, security, and privacy
TCO	Total cost of ownership
TCP	Transmission control protocol
UQC	Universal quantum computer
VC	Venture capital
VR	Virtual reality

VUI	Voice user interface
WAN	Wide area network
WCD	Wearable computing devices
WFH	Work from home
WHO	World Health Organization
ZTM	Zero trust model

Introduction

This book explores quantum computing as a transformative technology and its applications in cryptography, teleportation, IoT, AI, and blockchain, and also the futurist concept of quantum internet. The book explains the concept of dark, small, and thick data and clarifies what data lake is. Other exciting technologies like edge/fog computing, CDN, SDN, wearable technology, and IoE topics are discussed in detail in the book. Information security applications like the zero trust model and the use of AI and blockchain in cybersecurity are explored. Two of the most intriguing concepts in computing "affective computing and autonomic computing" are simplified in the book. Blockchain applications presented include blockchain and supply chain, crowdsourcing, cryptocurrency, and IoT. The book ends with a look at future trends in technology including the concept of metaverse.

PART 1

Quantum Computing

1

What is Quantum Computing?

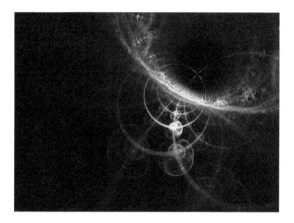

Quantum computing is the area of study focused on developing computer technology based on the principles of quantum theory. The quantum computer, following the laws of quantum physics, would gain enormous processing power through the ability to be in multiple states and to perform tasks using all possible permutations simultaneously.

1.1 A Comparison of Classical and Quantum Computing

Classical computing relies, at its ultimate level, on principles expressed by the Boolean algebra. Data must be processed in an exclusive binary state at any point in time or bits. While the time that each transistor or capacitor needs to be either in 0 or 1 before switching states is now measurable in billionths of a second, there is still a limit as to how quickly these devices can be made to switch state. As we progress to smaller and faster circuits, we begin to reach the physical limits of materials and the threshold for classical laws of physics to apply. Beyond this, the quantum world takes over [1].

In a quantum computer, a number of elemental particles such as electrons or photons can be used with either their *charge* or *polarization* acting as a representation of 0 and/or 1. Each of these particles is known as a quantum bit, or *qubit*; the nature and behavior of these particles form the basis of quantum computing.

1.2 Quantum Superposition and Entanglement

The two most relevant aspects of quantum physics are the principles of *superposition* and *entanglement*.

Superposition: Think of a qubit as an electron in a magnetic field. The electron's spin may be either in alignment with the field, which is known as a spin-up state, or opposite to the field, which is known as a spin-down state. According to quantum law, the particle enters a superposition of states, in which it behaves as if it were in both states simultaneously. Each qubit utilized could take a superposition of both 0 and 1.

Entanglement: Particles that have interacted at some point retain a type of connection and can be entangled with each other in pairs, in a process known as *correlation*. Knowing the spin state of one entangled particle – up or down – allows one to know that the spin of its mate is in the opposite direction. Quantum entanglement allows qubits that are separated by incredible distances to interact with each other instantaneously (not limited to the speed of light). No matter how great the distance between the correlated particles is, they will remain entangled as long as they are isolated.

Taken together, quantum superposition and entanglement create an enormously enhanced computing power. While a 2-bit register in an ordinary computer can store only one of four binary configurations (00, 01, 10, or 11) at any given time, a 2-qubit register in a quantum computer can store all four numbers simultaneously, because each qubit represents two values. If more qubits are added, the increased capacity is expanded exponentially [2].

1.3 Difficulties with Quantum Computers

• *Interference*: During the computation phase of a quantum calculation, the slightest disturbance in a quantum system (say a stray photon or wave of EM radiation) causes the quantum computation to collapse, a process known as *de-coherence*. A quantum computer must be totally isolated from all external interference during the computation phase.

- *Error correction*: Given the nature of quantum computing, error correction is ultra-critical; even a single error in a calculation can cause the validity of the entire computation to collapse.

- *Output observance*: Closely related to the above two, retrieving output data after a quantum calculation is complete risks corrupting the data [3].

1.4 The Future of Quantum Computing

The biggest and the most important one is the ability to factorize a very large number into two prime numbers. That is really important because that is what almost all *encryptions* of internet applications use and can be de-encrypted. A quantum computer should be able to do that relatively quickly. For example calculating the positions of individual atoms in very large molecules like polymers and in viruses. The way that the particles interact with each other – if you have a quantum computer, you could use it to develop drugs and understand how molecules work a bit better.

Even though there are many problems to overcome, the breakthroughs in the last 15 years, and especially in the last 3 years, have made some form of practical quantum computing possible. However, the potential that this technology offers is attracting tremendous interest from both the government and the private sectors. It is this potential that is rapidly breaking down the barriers to this technology, but whether all barriers can be broken, and when, is very much an open question [4, 5].

References

[1] http://www.fastcolabs.com/3013214/why-quantum-computing-is-faster-for-everything-but-the-web
[2] http://www.theguardian.com/science/2014/mar/06/quantum-computing-explained-particle-mechanics
[3] http://www.economist.com/news/science-and-technology/21578027-first-real-world-contests-between-quantum-computers-and-standard-ones-faster
[4] http://whatis.techtarget.com/definition/quantum-computing
[5] http://physics.about.com/od/quantumphysics/f/quantumcomp.htm

2

Quantum Cryptography

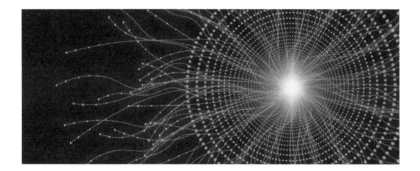

Quantum cryptography uses physics to develop a cryptosystem completely secure against being compromised without knowledge of the sender or the receiver of the messages. The word *quantum* itself refers to the most fundamental behavior of the smallest particles of matter and energy.

Quantum cryptography is different from traditional cryptographic systems in that it relies more on physics, rather than mathematics, as a key aspect of its security model [7].

Essentially, quantum cryptography is based on the usage of individual particles/waves of light (photon) and their intrinsic quantum properties to develop an unbreakable cryptosystem (*because it is impossible to measure the quantum state of any system without disturbing that system*).

Quantum cryptography uses photons to transmit a key. Once the key is transmitted, coding and encoding using the normal secret-key method can take place. But how does a photon become a key? How do you attach information to a photon's spin [8]?

This is where *binary code* comes into play. Each type of a photon's spin represents one piece of information – usually a 1 or a 0, for binary code. This code uses strings of 1s and 0s to create a coherent message. For example, 11100100110 could correspond with h-e-l-l-o. So a binary code can be assigned to each photon – for example, a photon that has a *vertical spin (|)* can be assigned a 1.

"If you build it correctly, no hacker can hack the system. The question is what it means to build it correctly," said physicist Renato Renner from the Institute of Theoretical Physics in Zurich [9].

Regular, non-quantum encryption can work in a variety of ways, but, generally, a message is scrambled and can only be unscrambled using a secret key. The trick is to make sure that whomever you are trying to hide your communication from does not get their hands on your secret key. Cracking the private key in a modern cryptosystem would generally require figuring out the factors of a number that is the product of two insanely huge prime numbers. The numbers are chosen to be so large that, with the given processing power of computers, it would take longer than the lifetime of the universe for an algorithm to factor their product.

But such encryption techniques have their vulnerabilities. Certain products – called weak keys – happen to be easier to factor than others. Also, Moore's law continually ups the processing power of our computers. Even more importantly, mathematicians are constantly developing new algorithms that allow for easier factorization.

Quantum cryptography avoids all these issues. Here, the key is encrypted into a series of photons that get passed between two parties trying to share secret information. The Heisenberg uncertainty principle dictates that an adversary cannot look at these photons without changing or destroying them.

"In this case, it doesn't matter what technology the adversary has, they'll never be able to break the laws of physics," said physicist Richard Hughes of Los Alamos National Laboratory in New Mexico, who works on quantum cryptography [10].

2.1 Problems with using Quantum Cryptography

But, in practice, quantum cryptography comes with its own load of weaknesses. It was recognized in 2010, for instance, that a hacker could blind a detector with a strong pulse, rendering it unable to see the secret-keeping photons.

Renner points to many other problems. Photons are often generated using a laser tuned to such a low intensity that it is producing one single photon at a time. There is a certain probability that the laser will make a photon encoded with your secret information and then a second photon with that same information. In this case, all an enemy has to do is steal that second photon and they could gain access to your data while you would be none the wiser.

Alternatively, noticing when a single photon has arrived can be tricky. Detectors might not register that a particle has hit them, making you think that your system has been hacked when it is really quite secure [11].

"If we had better control over quantum systems than we have with today's technology then perhaps quantum cryptography could be less susceptible to problems,: said Renner. But such advances are at least 10 years away.

Still, he added, no system is 100% perfect and even more advanced technology will always deviate from theory in some ways. A clever hacker will always find a way to exploit such security holes.

Any encryption method will only be *as secure as the humans running it*, added Hughes. Whenever someone claims that a particular technology "is fundamentally unbreakable, people will say that's snake oil," he said. "Nothing is unbreakable" [12].

References

[6] http://www.qi.damtp.cam.ac.uk/node/38

[7] http://www.businessinsider.com/what-is-quantum-encryption-2014-3#ixzz33jYuMw48

[8] http://www.wired.com/2013/06/quantum-cryptography-hack/

[9] http://searchsecurity.techtarget.com/definition/quantum-cryptography

[10] http://science.howstuffworks.com/science-vs-myth/everyday-myths/quantum-cryptology.htm

[11] http://www.wisegeek.com/what-is-quantum-cryptography.htm

[12] http://www.techrepublic.com/blog/it-security/how-quantum-cryptography-works-and-by-the-way-its-breakable/

3

Quantum Internet

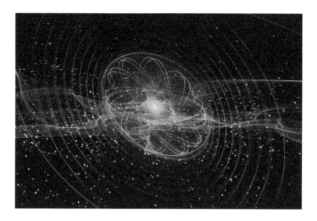

Building a quantum internet is a key ambition for many countries around the world; such a breakthrough will give them competitive advantage in a promising disruptive technology and opens a new world of innovations and unlimited possibilities.

Recently, the US Department of Energy (DoE) published the first blueprint of its kind, laying out a step-by-step strategy to make the quantum internet dream come true. The main goal is to make it impervious to any cyber hacking. It will "metamorphosize our entire way of life," says the Department of Energy. Nearly $625 million in federal funding is expected to be allocated to the project.

A quantum internet would be able to transmit large volumes of data across immense distances at a rate that exceeds the *speed of light*. You can imagine all the applications that can benefit from such speed.

Traditional computer data is coded in either zeros or ones. Quantum information is superimposed in both zeros and ones simultaneously. Academics, researchers, and IT professionals will need to create devices for the infrastructure of quantum internet including: quantum routers, repeaters, gateways, hubs, and other quantum tools. A whole new industry will be born based on the idea that quantum internet exists in parallel to the current eco-system of companies we have in regular internet.

The "traditional internet," as the regular internet is sometimes called, will still exist. It is expected that large organizations will rely on the quantum internet to safeguard data, but those individual consumers will continue to use the classical internet [13].

Experts predict that the financial sector will benefit from the quantum internet when it comes to securing online transactions. The healthcare sectors and the public sectors are also expected to see benefits. In addition to providing a faster, safer internet experience, quantum computing will better position organizations to solve complex problems, like supply chain management. Furthermore, it will expedite the exchange of vast amounts of data, and carrying out large-scale sensing experiments in astronomy, materials discovery and life sciences [13, 15].

But first let us explain some of the basic terms of the quantum world: Quantum computing is the area of study focused on developing computer technology based on the principles of *quantum theory*. The quantum computer, following the laws of quantum physics, would gain *enormous processing power* through the ability to be in multiple states and to perform tasks using all possible permutations simultaneously [14].

In a quantum computer, a number of elemental particles such as *electrons or photons* can be used with either their *charge* or *polarization* acting as a representation of 0 and/or 1. Each of these particles is known as a *quantum bit*, or *qubit*; the nature and behavior of these particles form the basis of quantum computing [14].

3.1 What is Quantum Internet?

The quantum internet is a network that will let quantum devices exchange some information within an environment that harnesses the odd laws of quantum mechanics. In theory, this would lend the quantum internet unprecedented capabilities that are impossible to carry out with today's web applications.

In the quantum world, data can be encoded in the state of qubits, which can be created in quantum devices like a quantum computer or a quantum processor. And the quantum internet, in simple terms, will involve sending qubits across a network of multiple quantum devices that are physically separated. Crucially, all of this would happen, thanks to the wild properties that are unique to quantum states.

That might sound similar to the standard internet. But sending qubits around through a quantum channel, rather than a classical one, effectively means leveraging the behavior of particles when taken at their smallest scale – so-called "quantum states."

Unsurprisingly, qubits cannot be used to send the kind of data we are familiar with, like emails and WhatsApp messages. But the strange behavior of qubits is opening up huge opportunities in other, more niche applications [13].

3.2 Quantum Communications

One of the most exciting avenues that researchers, armed with qubits, are exploring is communications *security* [13].

Quantum security leads us to the concept of *quantum cryptography* which uses physics to develop a cryptosystem completely secure against being compromised without the knowledge of the sender or the receiver of the messages.

Essentially, quantum cryptography is based on the usage of individual particles/waves of light (photon) and their intrinsic quantum properties to develop an unbreakable cryptosystem (*because it is impossible to measure the quantum state of any system without disturbing that system*) [16].

Quantum cryptography uses photons to transmit a key. Once the key is transmitted, coding and encoding using the normal secret-key method can take place. But how does a photon become a key? How do you attach information to a photon's spin [16]?

This is where binary code comes into play. Each type of a photon's spin represents one piece of information – usually a 1 or a 0, for binary code. This code uses strings of 1s and 0s to create a coherent message. For example, 11100100110 could correspond with h-e-l-l-o. So a binary code can be assigned to each photon – for example, a photon that has a vertical spin (|) can be assigned a 1.

Regular, non-quantum encryption can work in a variety of ways, but generally a message is scrambled and can only be unscrambled using a secret key. The trick is to make sure that whomever you are trying to hide your communication from does not get their hands on your secret key. But such encryption techniques have their vulnerabilities. Certain products – called weak keys – happen to be easier to factor than others. Also, Moore's law continually ups the processing power of our computers. Even more importantly, mathematicians are constantly developing new algorithms that allow for easier factorization of the secret key [16].

Quantum cryptography avoids all these issues. Here, the key is encrypted into a series of photons that get passed between two parties trying to share secret information. The Heisenberg uncertainty principle dictates that an adversary cannot look at these photons without changing or destroying them [16].

References

[13] https://www.cybertalk.org/2020/10/23/quantum-internet-fast-forward-into-the-future/

[14] https://www.bbvaopenmind.com/en/technology/digital-world/quantum-computing/

[15] https://www.zdnet.com/article/what-is-the-quantum-internet-everything-you-need-to-know-about-the-weird-future-of-quantum-networks/

[16] https://ahmedbanafa.blogspot.com/2014/06/understanding-quantum-cryptography.html

4

Quantum Teleportation

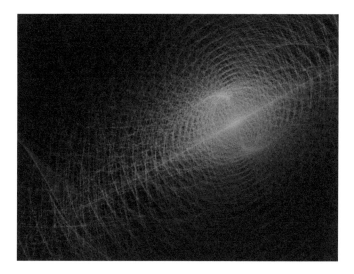

Quantum teleportation is a technique for transferring quantum information from a sender at one location to a receiver some distance away. While teleportation is commonly portrayed in science fiction as a means to transfer physical objects from one location to the next, quantum teleportation only transfers *quantum information*. An interesting note is that the sender knows neither the location of the recipient nor the quantum state that will be transferred [17].

For the first time, a team of scientists and researchers have achieved sustained, high-fidelity "quantum teleportation" – the instant transfer of "qubits," the basic unit of quantum information. The collaborative team, which includes NASA's jet propulsion laboratory, successfully demonstrated sustained, long-distance teleportation of qubits of photons (quanta of light) with fidelity greater than 90%. The qubits (quantum bits) were teleported 44 kilometers (27 miles) over a fiber-optic network using state-of-the-art single-photon detectors and off-the-shelf equipment [20].

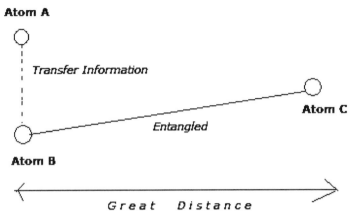

Figure 4.1   Quantum entanglement.

Quantum teleportation is the transfer of quantum states from one location to another. Through quantum entanglement, two particles in separate locations are connected by an invisible force, famously referred to as "*spooky action at a distance*" by Albert Einstein. Regardless of the distance, the encoded information shared by the "entangled" pair of particles can be passed between them [20].

By sharing these quantum qubits, the basic units of quantum computing, researchers are hoping to create networks of quantum computers that can share information at blazing-fast speeds. But keeping this information flow stable over long distances has proven extremely difficult. Researchers are now hoping to scale up such a system, using both entanglement to send information and quantum memory to store it as well [20].

On the same front, researchers have advanced their quantum technology research works with a chip that could be scaled up and used to build the quantum simulator of the future using nanochip that allows them to produce enough stable photons encoded with quantum information to scale up the technology. The chip, which is said to be less than one-tenth of the thickness of a human hair, may enable the researchers to achieve "quantum supremacy" – where a quantum device can solve a given computational task faster than the world's most powerful supercomputer [20].

But first let us explain some of the basic terms of the quantum world: Quantum computing is the area of study focused on developing computer technology based on the principles of *quantum theory*. The quantum computer, following the laws of quantum physics, would gain *enormous processing power* through the ability to be in multiple states, and to perform tasks using all possible permutations simultaneously [18].

4.1 Quantum Teleportation: Paving the Way for a Quantum Internet

In July, the US Department of Energy unveiled a blueprint for the first quantum internet, connecting several of its national laboratories across the country. A quantum internet would be able to transmit large volumes of data across immense distances at a rate that exceeds the speed of light. You can imagine all the applications that can benefit from such speed [18].

Traditional computer data is coded in either zeros or ones. Quantum information is superimposed in both zeros and ones simultaneously. Academics, researchers, and IT professionals will need to create devices for the infrastructure of quantum internet including: quantum routers, repeaters, gateways, hubs, and other quantum tools. A whole new industry will be born based on the idea that quantum internet exists in parallel to the current ecosystem of companies we have in regular internet [18].

The "traditional internet," as the regular internet is sometimes called, will still exist. It is expected that large organizations will rely on the quantum internet to safeguard data, but those individual consumers will continue to use the classical internet [18].

Experts predict that the financial sector will benefit from the quantum internet when it comes to securing online transactions. The healthcare sectors and the public sectors are also expected to see benefits. In addition to providing a faster, safer internet experience, quantum computing will better position organizations to solve complex problems, like supply chain management. Furthermore, it will expedite the exchange of vast amounts of data and carrying out large-scale sensing experiments in astronomy, materials discovery, and life sciences [18].

References

[17] https://en.wikipedia.org/wiki/Quantum_teleportation
[18] https://www.linkedin.com/pulse/quantum-internet-explained-ahmed-banafa/
[19] https://www.designboom.com/technology/nasa-long-distance-quantum-teleportation-12-22-2020/
[20] https://www.siliconrepublic.com/machines/quantum-computing-fermilab

5

Quantum Computing and IoT

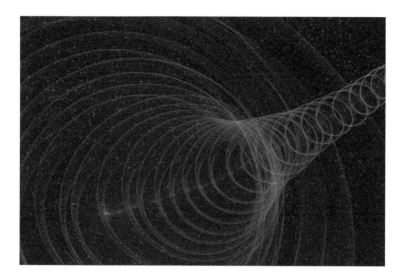

Consumers, companies, and governments will install 40 billion IoT devices globally. Smart tech finds its way to every business and consumer domain there is – from retail to healthcare and from finances to logistics – and a missed opportunity strategically employed by a competitor can easily qualify as a long-term failure for companies who do not innovate.

Moreover, the 2020's challenges just confirmed the need to secure all four components of the IoT model: sensors, networks (communications), analytics (cloud), and applications [21, 23].

One of the top candidates to help in securing IoT is quantum computing, while the idea of convergence of IoT and quantum computing is not a new topic; it was discussed in many works of literature and covered by various researchers, but nothing is close to practical applications so far. Quantum computing is not ready yet; it is years away from deployment on a commercial scale.

To understand the complexity of this kind of convergence, first, you need to recognize the security issues of IoT, and, second, comprehend the complicated nature of quantum computing.

IoT system's diverse security issues include [4, 5, 7]:

- *Data breaches*: IoT applications collect a lot of user data, and most of it is sensitive or personal, to operate and function correctly. As such, it needs encryption protection.

- *Data authentication*: Some devices may have adequate encryption in place, but it can still be open to hackers if the authenticity of the data that is communicated to and from the IoT device cannot be authenticated.

- *Side-channel attacks*: Certain attacks focus on the data and information it can gain from a system's implementation rather than vulnerabilities in the implementation's algorithms.

- *Irregular updates*: Due to the rapid advances in the IoT industry, a device that may have been secure on its release may not be secure anymore if its software does not get updated regularly. Add to that the famous SolarWinds's Supply Chain attack of 2020 which infected over 18,000 companies and government agencies using updates of office applications, and network monitoring tools.

- *Malware and ransomware*: Malware refers to the multitude of malicious programs that typically infect a device and influence its functioning, whereas ransomware has the capabilities to lock a user out of their device, usually requesting a "ransom" to gain full use back again paid by cryptocurrency "bitcoin."

5.1 A Comparison of Classical and Quantum Computing

Classical computing relies, at its ultimate level, on principles expressed by a branch of math called the Boolean algebra. Data must be processed in an exclusive binary state at any point in time or bits. While the time that each transistor or capacitor needs to be either in 0 or 1 before switching states is now measurable in billionths of a second, there is still a limit as to how quickly these devices can be made to switch state. As we progress to smaller and faster circuits, we begin to reach the physical limits of materials and the threshold for classical laws of physics to apply. Beyond this, the quantum world takes over.

In a quantum computer, several elemental particles such as electrons or photons can be used with either their charge or polarization acting as a representation of 0 and/or 1. Each of these particles is known as a quantum bit, or qubit; the nature and behavior of these particles form the basis of quantum computing [22].

5.2 Quantum Communications

One of the most exciting avenues that researchers, armed with qubits, are exploring is communications security.

Quantum security leads us to the concept of *quantum cryptography* which uses physics to develop a cryptosystem completely secure against being compromised without the knowledge of the sender or the receiver of the messages.

Essentially, quantum cryptography is based on the usage of individual particles/waves of light (photon) and their intrinsic quantum properties to develop an unbreakable cryptosystem (because it is impossible to measure the quantum state of any system without disturbing that system).

Quantum cryptography uses photons to transmit a key. Once the key is transmitted, coding and encoding using the normal secret-key method can take place. But how does a photon become a key? How do you attach information to a photon's spin?

This is where binary code comes into play. Each type of a photon's spin represents one piece of information – usually a 1 or a 0, for binary code. This code uses strings of 1s and 0s to create a coherent message. For example, 11100100110 could correspond with h-e-l-l-o. So a binary code can be assigned to each photon – for example, a photon that has a vertical spin (|) can be assigned a 1.

Regular, non-quantum encryption can work in a variety of ways, but, generally, a message is scrambled and can only be unscrambled using a secret key. The trick is to make sure that whomever you are trying to hide your communication from does not get their hands on your secret key. But such encryption techniques have their vulnerabilities. Certain products – called weak keys – happen to be easier to factor than others. Also, Moore's law continually ups the processing power of our computers. Even more importantly, mathematicians are constantly developing new algorithms that allow for easier factorization of the secret key.

Quantum cryptography avoids all these issues. Here, the key is encrypted into a series of photons that get passed between two parties trying to share secret information. Heisenberg's uncertainty principle dictates that an adversary cannot look at these photons without changing or destroying them [22, 24].

5.3 Quantum Computing and IoT

With its capabilities, quantum computing can help address the challenges and issues that hamper the growth of IoT. Some of these capabilities are as follows [3]:

- *Optimized complex computation power*: With quantum computing, the speed is incredibly high; IoT benefits from this speed since IoT devices generate a massive amount of data that requires heavy computation and other complex optimization.

- *Faster validation and verification process*: Quantum computing addresses that concern as it can speed up the verification and validation process across all the systems several times faster while ensuring constant optimization of the systems.

- *More secure communications*: A more secure communication is possible through *quantum cryptography* as explained before. The complexity serves as a defense against cyberattacks including data breaches, authentication, malware, and ransomware.

5.4 The Road Ahead

Quantum computing is still in its development stage with tech giants such as IBM, Google, and Microsoft putting in resources to build powerful quantum computers. While they were able to build machines containing more and more qubits, for example, Google announced in 2019 that they achieved "quantum supremacy." The challenge is to get these qubits to operate smoothly and with less error. But with the technology being very promising, continuous research and development are expected until such time that it reaches widespread practical applications for both consumers and businesses [23, 26].

IoT is expanding as we depend on our digital devices more every day. Furthermore, work from home (WFH) concept that resulted from COVID-19 lockdowns accelerated the deployment of many IoT devices and shortened the learning curves of using such devices. When IoT converges with quantum computing under "quantum IoT" or QIoT, which will push other technologies to use quantum computing and add "quantum" or "Q" to their product and service labels, we will see more adoption of quantum hardware and software applications in addition to quantum services like QSaaS, QIaaS, and QPaaS as parts of quantum cloud and quantum artificial intelligence (QAI) to mention few examples [25, 27].

References

[21] https://ahmedbanafa.blogspot.com/2019/12/ten-trends-of-iot-in-2020.html

[22] https://ahmedbanafa.blogspot.com/2020/11/quantum-internet-explained.html

[23] https://www.azoquantum.com/Article.aspx?ArticleID=101

[24] https://www.cybersecurityintelligence.com/blog/quantum-computing-the-internet-of-things-and-hackers-4914.html

[25] https://www.europeanbusinessreview.com/iot-security-are-we-ready-for-a-quantum-world/

[26] https://www.bbvaopenmind.com/en/technology/digital-world/quantum-computing-and-blockchain-facts-and-myths/

[27] https://www.ft.com/content/c13dbb51-907b-4db7-8347-30921ef

6

Quantum Computing and Blockchain: Myths and Facts

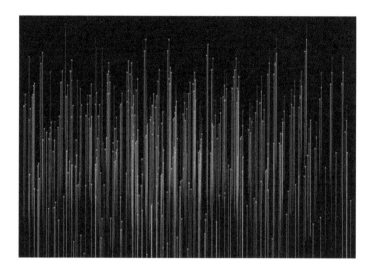

The biggest danger to blockchain networks from quantum computing is its ability to break traditional encryption [30].

Google sent shock waves around the internet when it was claimed and had built a quantum computer able to solve formerly impossible mathematical calculations – with some fearing crypto industry could be at risk. Google states that its experiment is the first experimental challenge against the *extended Church–Turing thesis* – also known as computability thesis – which claims that traditional computers can effectively carry out any "reasonable" model of computation

6.1 Difficulties with Quantum Computers [31]

* *Interference*: During the computation phase of a quantum calculation, the slightest disturbance in a quantum system (say a stray photon or

wave of EM radiation) causes the quantum computation to collapse, a process known as *de-coherence*. A quantum computer must be totally isolated from all external interference during the computation phase.

- *Error correction*: Given the nature of quantum computing, error correction is ultra-critical – even a single error in a calculation can cause the validity of the entire computation to collapse.

- *Output observance*: Closely related to the above two, retrieving output data after a quantum calculation is complete risks corrupting the data.

6.2 What Is Quantum Supremacy?

According to the *Financial Times*, Google claims to have successfully built the world's most powerful quantum computer. What that means, according to Google's researchers, is that calculations that normally take more than 10,000 years to perform could be done by Google's computer in about *200 seconds*, and potentially mean blockchain, and the encryption that underpins it, could be broken.

Asymmetric cryptography used in crypto relies on key pairs, namely a private and public key. Public keys can be calculated from their private counterpart, but *not* the other way around. This is due to the impossibility of certain mathematical problems. Quantum computers are more efficient in accomplishing this by magnitudes, and if the calculation is done the other way, then the whole scheme breaks [30].

It would appear that Google is still some way away from building a quantum computer that could be a threat to blockchain cryptography or other encryption.

"Google's supercomputer currently has 53 qubits," said Dragos Ilie, a quantum computing and encryption researcher at Imperial College London.

"In order to have any effect on bitcoin or most other financial systems it would take at least about 1500 qubits and the system must allow for the entanglement of all of them," said Ilie.

Meanwhile, scaling quantum computers is "a huge challenge," according to Ilie [28].

Blockchain networks including bitcoin's architecture relies on two algorithms: elliptic curve digital signature algorithm (ECDSA) for digital signatures and SHA-256 as a hash function. A quantum computer could use Shor's algorithm [8] to get your private from your public key, but the most optimistic scientific estimates say that even if this were possible, it will not happen during this decade.

"A 160 bit elliptic curve cryptographic key could be broken on a quantum computer using around *1000 qubits* while factoring the security-wise equivalent 1024 bit RSA modulus would require about *2000 qubits*." By comparison, Google's measly 53 qubits are still no match for this kind of cryptography. According to research paper on the matter published by Cornell University.

But that is not to say that there is no cause for alarm. While the native encryption algorithms used by blockchain's applications are safe for now, the fact is that the rate of advancements in quantum technology is increasing, and that could, in time, pose a threat. "We expect their computational power will continue to grow at a double exponential rate," said Google researchers.

6.3 What is Quantum Cryptography?

Quantum cryptography uses physics to develop a cryptosystem completely secure against being compromised without the knowledge of the sender or the receiver of the messages. The word quantum itself refers to the most fundamental behavior of the smallest particles of matter and energy.

Quantum cryptography is different from traditional cryptographic systems in that it relies more on physics, rather than on mathematics, as a key aspect of its security model.

Essentially, quantum cryptography is based on the usage of individual particles/waves of light (photon) and their intrinsic quantum properties to develop an unbreakable cryptosystem (*because it is impossible to measure the quantum state of any system without disturbing that system*).

Quantum cryptography uses photons to transmit a key. Once the key is transmitted, coding and encoding using the normal secret-key method can take place. But how does a photon become a key? How do you attach information to a photon's spin?

This is where *binary code* comes into play. Each type of a photon's spin represents one piece of information – usually a 1 or a 0, for binary code. This code uses strings of 1s and 0s to create a coherent message. For example, 11100100110 could correspond with h-e-l-l-o. So a binary code can be assigned to each photon – for example, a photon that has a *vertical spin* (|) can be assigned a 1.

"If you build it correctly, no hacker can hack the system. The question is what it means to build it correctly," said physicist Renato Renner from the Institute of Theoretical Physics in Zurich.

Regular, non-quantum encryption can work in a variety of ways, but, generally, a message is scrambled and can only be unscrambled using a secret key. The trick is to make sure that whomever you are trying to hide your communication from does not get their hands on your secret key. Cracking the private key in a modern cryptosystem would generally require figuring out the factors of a number that is the product of two insanely huge prime numbers.

The numbers are chosen to be so large that, with the given processing power of computers, it would take longer than the lifetime of the universe for an algorithm to factor their product.

Encryption techniques have their vulnerabilities. Certain products – called weak keys – happen to be easier to factor than others. Also, Moore's law continually ups the processing power of our computers. Even more importantly, mathematicians are constantly developing new algorithms that allow for easier factorization.

Quantum cryptography avoids all these issues. Here, the key is encrypted into a series of photons that get passed between two parties trying to share secret information. The Heisenberg uncertainty principle dictates that an adversary cannot look at these photons without changing or destroying them.

"In this case, it doesn't matter what technology the adversary has, they'll never be able to break the laws of physics," said physicist Richard Hughes of Los Alamos National Laboratory in New Mexico, who works on quantum cryptography [32, 33].

References

[28] https://www.forbes.com/sites/billybambrough/2019/10/02/could-google-be-about-to-break-bitcoin/#1d78c5373329
[29] https://decrypt.co/9642/what-google-quantum-computer-means-for-bitcoin/
[30] https://www.coindesk.com/how-should-crypto-prepare-for-googles-quantum-supremacy?
[31] https://www.ccn.com/google-quantum-bitcoin/
[32] https://www.linkedin.com/pulse/20140503185010-246665791-quantum-computing/
[33] https://www.linkedin.com/pulse/20140608053056-246665791-under-standing-quantum-

7

Quantum Computing and AI:
A Mega-Buzzword

Quantum computers are designed to perform tasks much more accurately and efficiently than conventional computers, providing developers with a new tool for specific applications. It is clear in the short term that quantum computers will not replace their traditional counterparts; instead, they will require classical computers to support their specialized abilities, such as system optimization [35].

Both quantum computing and artificial intelligence are transformational technologies, and artificial intelligence needs quantum computing to achieve significant progress. Although artificial intelligence produces functional applications with classical computers, it is limited by the computational capabilities of classical computers. Quantum computing can provide a computation boost to artificial intelligence, enabling it to tackle more complex problems in many fields in business and science [37].

7.1 What is Quantum Computing?

Quantum computing is the area of study focused on developing computer technology based on the principles of quantum theory. The quantum computer, following the laws of quantum physics, would gain enormous processing power through the ability to be in multiple states, and to perform tasks using all possible permutations simultaneously.

7.2 Difficulties with Quantum Computers

- *Interference*: During the computation phase of a quantum calculation, the slightest disturbance in a quantum system (say a stray photon or wave of EM radiation) causes the quantum computation to collapse, a process known as *de-coherence*. A quantum computer must be totally isolated from all external interference during the computation phase.

- *Error correction*: Given the nature of quantum computing, error correction is ultra-critical – even a single error in a calculation can cause the validity of the entire computation to collapse.

- *Output observance*: Closely related to the above two, retrieving output data after a quantum calculation is complete risks corrupting the data.

7.3 Applications of Quantum Computing and AI

Keeping in mind that the term "quantum AI" means the use of quantum computing for computation of machine learning algorithms, which takes advantage of computational superiority of quantum computing, to achieve results that are not possible to achieve with classical computers, the following are some of the applications of this super mix of quantum computing and AI [34, 37]:

7.4 Processing Large Sets of Data

We produce 2.5 exabytes of data every day. That is equivalent to 250,000 Libraries of Congress or the content of 5 million laptops. Every minute of every day, 3.2 billion global internet users continue to feed the data banks with 9722 pins on Pinterest, 347,222 tweets, 4.2 million Facebook likes plus *all* the other data we create by taking pictures and videos, saving documents, opening accounts, and more [36].

Quantum computers are designed to manage the huge amount of data, along with uncovering patterns and spotting anomalies extremely quickly. With each newly launched iteration of quantum computer design and the new improvements made on the quantum error-correction code, developers are now able to better manage the potential of quantum bits. Also it

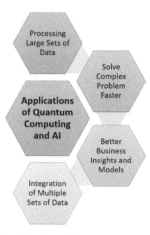

Figure 7.1 Applications of quantum computing and AI.

optimizes the same for solving all kinds of business problems to make better decisions [35].

7.5 Solve Complex Problem Faster

Quantum computers can complete calculations within seconds, which would take today's computers many years to calculate. With quantum computing, developers can do multiple calculations with multiple inputs simultaneously. Quantum computers are critical to process the monumental amount of data that businesses generate on a daily basis, and the fast calculation can be used to solve very complex problems which can be expressed as quantum supremacy where the calculations that normally take more than 10,000 years to perform could be done by a quantum computer in *200 seconds*. The key is to translate real-world problems that companies are facing into quantum language [35, 39].

7.6 Better Business Insights and Models

With the increasing amount of data generated in industries like pharmaceutical, finance, and life science industry, companies are losing their ties with classical computing rope. To have a better data framework, these companies now require complex models that have the potential processing power to model the most complex situations. And that is where quantum computers play a huge role creating better models with quantum technology will lead to better treatments for diseases in the healthcare sector like COVID-19 research cycle from test; tracing and treating of the virus can decrease financial implosion in the banking sector and improve the logistics chain in the manufacturing industry [35].

7.7 Integration of Multiple Sets of Data

To manage and integrate multiple numbers of sets of data from multiple sources, quantum computers is best to help, which makes the process quicker and also makes the analysis easier. The ability to handle so many stakes make quantum computing an adequate choice for solving business problems in a variety of fields [35].

7.8 The Future

The quantum computing market will reach \$2.2 Billion, and the number of installed quantum computers will reach around 180 in 2026, with about 45 machines produced in that year. These include both machines installed at the quantum computer companies themselves that are accessed by quantum services as well as customer premise machines [38].

Cloud access revenues will likely dominate as a revenue source for quantum computing companies in the format of quantum computing as a service (QCaaS) offering, which will be accounting for 75% of all quantum computing revenues in 2026. Although in the long run quantum computers may be more widely purchased, today, potential end users are more inclined to do quantum computing over the cloud rather than making technologically risky and expensive investments in quantum computing equipment [38].

In a parallel track, quantum software applications, developers' tools, and number of quantum engineers and experts will grow as the infrastructure developed over the next 5 years which will make it possible for more organizations to harvest the power of two transformational technologies, quantum computing and AI, and encourage many universities to add quantum computing as an essential part of their curriculum.

References

[34] https://www.linkedin.com/pulse/quantum-computing-blockchain-facts-myths-ahmed-banafa/
[35] https://analyticsindiamag.com/will-quantum-computing-define-the-future-of-ai/

[36] https://www.analyticsinsight.net/ai-quantum-computing-can-enable-much-anticipated-advancements/

[37] https://research.aimultiple.com/quantum-ai/

[38] https://www.globenewswire.com/news-release/2020/11/17/2128495/0/en/Quantum-Computing-Market-is-Expected-to-Reach-2-2-Billion-by-2026.html

[39] https://ai.googleblog.com/2019/10/quantum-supremacy-using-programmable.html

8

Quantum Computing Trends

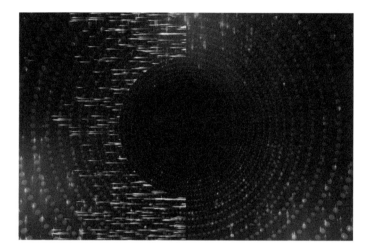

Quantum computing is the area of study focused on developing computer technology based on the principles of quantum theory. Tens of billions of public and private capitals are being invested in quantum technologies. Countries across the world have realized that quantum technologies can be a major disruptor of existing businesses; they have collectively invested $24 billion in quantum research and applications in 2021 [40].

8.1 A Comparison of Classical and Quantum Computing

Classical computing relies, at its ultimate level, on principles expressed by the Boolean algebra. Data must be processed in an exclusive binary state at any point in time or what we call bits. While the time that each transistor or capacitor needs to be either in 0 or 1 before switching states is now measurable in billionths of a second, there is still a limit as to how quickly these devices can be made to switch state.

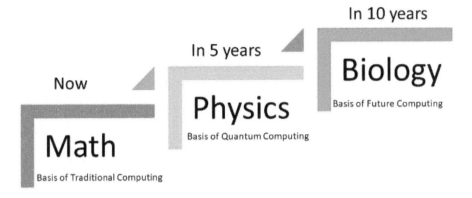

Future of Computing

Figure 8.1   Future of computing.

As we progress to smaller and faster circuits, we begin to reach the physical limits of materials and the threshold for classical laws of physics to apply. Beyond this, the quantum world takes over, in a quantum computer, a number of elemental particles such as electrons or photons that can be used with either their *charge* or *polarization* acting as a representation of 0 and/or 1. Each of these particles is known as a quantum bit, or *qubit*; the nature and behavior of these particles form the basis of quantum computing [2]. Classic computers use transistors as the physical building blocks of logic, while quantum computers may use trapped ions, superconducting loops, quantum dots, or vacancies in a diamond [40].

8.2 Physical vs. Logical Qubits

When discussing quantum computers with error correction, we talk about physical and logical qubits. Physical qubits are the physical qubits in quantum computer, whereas logical qubits are groups of physical qubits that we use as a single qubit in our computation to fight noise and improve error correction.

To illustrate this, let us consider an example of a quantum computer with 100 qubits. Let us say this computer is prone to noise; to remedy this, we can use multiple qubits to form a single more stable qubit. We might decide that we need 10 physical qubits to form one acceptable logical qubit. In this case, we would say our quantum computer has 100 physical qubits which we use as 10 logical qubits.

Distinguishing between physical and logical qubits is important. There are many estimates as to how many qubits we will need to perform certain calculations, but some of these estimates talk about logical qubits and others talk about physical qubits. For example, to break RSA cryptography, we would need thousands of logical qubits but millions of physical qubits.

Another thing to keep in mind is that in a classical computer, compute-power increases linearly with the number of transistors and clock speed, while in a quantum computer, compute-power increases exponentially with the addition of each logical qubit [43].

8.3 Quantum Superposition and Entanglement

The two most relevant aspects of quantum physics are the principles of *superposition* and *entanglement.*

Superposition: Think of a qubit as an electron in a magnetic field. The electron's spin may be either in alignment with the field, which is known as a spin-up state, or opposite to the field, which is known as a spin-down state. According to quantum law, the particle enters a superposition of states, in which it behaves as if it were in both states simultaneously. Each qubit utilized could take a superposition of both 0 and 1. Here, a 2-bit register in an ordinary computer can store only one of four binary configurations (00, 01, 10, or 11) at any given time, and a 2-qubit register in a quantum computer can store all four numbers simultaneously, because each qubit represents two values. If more qubits are added, the increased capacity is expanded exponentially.

Entanglement: Particles that have interacted at some point retain a type of connection and can be entangled with each other in pairs, in a process known as correlation. Knowing the spin state of one entangled particle – up or down – allows one to know that the spin of its mate is in the opposite direction. Quantum entanglement allows qubits that are separated by incredible distances to interact with each other instantaneously (not limited to the speed of light). No matter how great the distance between the correlated particles

Figure 8.2 Quantum computuers categories.

is, they will remain entangled as long as they are isolated. Taken together, quantum superposition and entanglement create an enormously enhanced computing power [42].

Quantum computers fall into four categories [40]:

1.   Quantum emulator/simulator

2.   Quantum annealer

3.   Noisy intermediate scale quantum (NISQ)

4.   Universal quantum computer – which can be a cryptographically relevant quantum computer (CRQC)

8.4 Quantum Emulator/Simulator

These are classical computers that you can buy today which simulate quantum algorithms. They make it easy to test and debug a quantum algorithm that someday may be able to run on a universal quantum computer (UQC). Since they do not use any quantum hardware, they are no faster than standard computers.

8.5 Quantum Annealer

Quantum annealer is a special purpose quantum computer designed to only run combinatorial optimization problems, not general-purpose computing, or cryptography problems. While they have more physical qubits than any other current system, they are not organized as gate-based logical qubits. Currently, this is a commercial technology in search of a future viable market.

8.6 Noisy Intermediate-Scale Quantum (NISQ) Computers

Think of these as *prototypes* of a universal quantum computer – with several orders of magnitude fewer bits. They currently have 50–100 qubits, limited gate depths, and short coherence times. As they are short several orders of magnitude of qubits, NISQ computers cannot perform any useful computation; however, they are a necessary phase in the learning, especially to drive total system and software learning in parallel to the hardware development. Think of them as the training wheels for future universal quantum computers.

8.7 Universal Quantum Computers/Cryptographically Relevant Quantum Computers (CRQC)

This is the ultimate goal. If you could build a universal quantum computer with fault tolerance (i.e., millions of error-corrected physical qubits resulting in thousands of logical qubits), you could run quantum algorithms in cryptography, search and optimization, quantum systems simulations, and linear equation solvers.

8.8 Post-Quantum/Quantum-Resistant Codes

New cryptographic systems would secure against both quantum and conventional computers and can interoperate with existing communication protocols and networks. The symmetric key algorithms of the commercial national security algorithm (CNSA) suite were selected to be secure for national security systems usage even if a CRQC is developed. Cryptographic schemes that commercial industry believes are quantum-safe include lattice-based cryptography, hash trees, multivariate equations, and super-singular isogeny elliptic curves [40].

8.9 Difficulties with Quantum Computers [41]

- *Interference*: During the computation phase of a quantum calculation, the slightest disturbance in a quantum system (say a stray photon or wave of EM radiation) causes the quantum computation to collapse, a process known as *de-coherence*. A quantum computer must be totally isolated from all external interference during the computation phase.

- *Error correction*: Given the nature of quantum computing, error correction is ultra-critical – even a single error in a calculation can cause the validity of the entire computation to collapse.

- *Output observance*: Closely related to the above two, retrieving output data after a quantum calculation is complete risks corrupting the data.

References

[40] https://www.linkedin.com/pulse/quantum-technology-ecosystem-explained-steve-blank/?

[41] https://www.bbvaopenmind.com/en/technology/digital-world/
    quantum-computing-and-ai/

[42] https://phys.org/news/2022-03-technique-quantum-resilient-noise-
    boosts.html

[43] https://thequantuminsider.com/2019/10/01/introduction-to-
    qubits-part-1/

PART 2

Other Computing Technologies

9

What is Deep Learning?

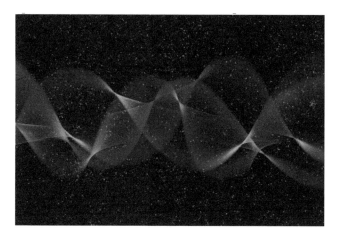

Deep learning is an emerging topic in artificial intelligence (AI). Being a subcategory of machine learning, deep learning deals with the use of *neural networks* to improve things like speech recognition, computer vision, and natural language processing. It is quickly becoming one of the most sought-after fields in computer science. In the last few years, deep learning has helped forge advances in areas as diverse as object perception, machine translation, and voice recognition – all research topics that have long been difficult for AI researchers to crack [49].

9.1 Neural Network

In information technology, a *neural network* is a system of programs and data structures that approximates the operation of the human brain. A neural network usually involves a large number of processors operating in parallel, each with its own small sphere of knowledge and access to data in its local memory. Typically, a neural network is initially "trained" or fed large amounts of data and rules about data relationships (for example, "A grand-father is older than a person's father"). A program can then tell the network how to behave in response to an external stimulus (for example, to input from a computer user who is interacting with the network) or can initiate activity on its own (within the limits of its access to the external world) [44, 45].

9.2 Deep Learning vs. Machine Learning

To understand what deep learning is, it is first important to distinguish it from other disciplines within the field of AI.

One outgrowth of AI was *machine learning*, in which the computer extracts knowledge through *supervised* experience. This typically involved a human operator helping the machine learn by giving it hundreds or thousands of training examples, and manually correcting its mistakes.

While machine learning has become dominant within the field of AI, it does have its problems. For one thing, it is massively time consuming. For another, it is still not a true measure of machine intelligence since it relies on human ingenuity to come up with the abstractions that allow computer to learn.

Unlike machine learning, deep learning is mostly *unsupervised*. It involves, for example, creating large-scale neural nets that allow the computer to learn and "think" by itself without the need for direct human intervention.

Deep learning "really doesn't look like a computer program," says Gary Marcus a psychologist and AI expert at New York University. He says ordinary computer code is written in very strict logical steps. "But what you'll see in deep learning is something different; you don't have a lot of instructions that say: 'If one thing is true do this other thing,'" he says. Instead of linear logic, deep learning is based on theories of how the human brain works. The program is made of tangled layers of interconnected nodes. It learns by rearranging connections between nodes after each new experience.

Deep learning has shown potential as the basis for software that could work out the emotions or events described in text even if they are not explicitly referenced, recognize objects in photos, and make sophisticated predictions about people's likely future behavior [46, 47].

9.3 The Deep Learning Game

In 2011, Google started *Google Brain* project, which created a neural network trained with deep learning algorithms, which famously proved capable of recognizing high level concepts.

Last year, Facebook established the *AI Research Unit*, using deep learning expertise to help create solutions that will better identify faces and objects in the *350 million* photos and videos uploaded to Facebook each day.

An example of deep learning in action is voice recognition like *Google Now* and Apple's *Siri*.

9.4 The Future

Deep learning is showing a great deal of promise, making self-driving cars and robotic butlers a real possibility. They are still limited, but what they can do was unthinkable just a few years ago, and it is advancing at an unprecedented pace. The ability to analyze massive datasets and use deep learning in computer systems that can adapt to experience, rather than depending on a human programmer, will lead to breakthroughs. These range from drug discovery to the development of new materials to robots with a greater awareness of the world around them. Maybe that will explain why Google has been on a buying spree lately, and robotics companies have been at the top of its shopping list. They have purchased *eight* robotics companies in a matter of months [48, 50].

References

[44] http://www.technologyreview.com/news/524026/is-google-cornering-the-market-on-deep-learning/

[45] http://www.forbes.com/sites/netapp/2013/08/19/what-is-deep-learning/

[46] http://www.fastcolabs.com/3026423/why-google-is-investing-in-deep-learning

[47] http://www.npr.org/blogs/alltechconsidered/2014/02/20/280232074/deep-learning-teaching-computers-to-tell-things-apart

[48] http://www.technologyreview.com/news/519411/facebook-launches-advanced-ai-effort-to-find-meaning-in-your-posts/

[49] http://www.deeplearning.net/tutorial/

[50] http://searchnetworking.techtarget.com/definition/neural-network

10

Affective Computing

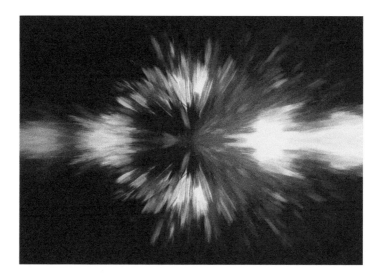

Affective computing is the study and development of systems and devices that can recognize, interpret, process, and simulate human affects. It is an interdisciplinary field spanning computer science, psychology, and cognitive science. While the origins of the field may be traced as far back as to early philosophical inquiries into emotion ("affect" is, basically, a synonym for "emotion"), the more modern branch of computer science originated with *Rosalind Picard's* 1995 paper on affective computing. A motivation for the research is the ability to simulate *empathy*. The machine should interpret the emotional state of humans and adapt its behavior to them, giving an appropriate response for those emotions [51].

Affective computing technologies sense the emotional state of a user (via sensors, microphone, cameras, and/or software logic) and respond by performing specific, predefined product/service features, such as changing a quiz or recommending a set of videos to fit the mood of the learner.

The more computers we have in our lives, the more we are going to want them to behave politely, and be socially smart. We do not want it to bother us with unimportant information. That kind of common-sense reasoning requires an understanding of the person's *emotional state* [51].

One way to look at affective computing is *human–computer interaction* in which a device has the ability to detect and appropriately respond to its user's emotions and other stimuli. A computing device with this capacity could gather cues to user emotion from a variety of sources. Facial expressions, posture, gestures, speech, the force or rhythm of key strokes, and the temperature changes of the hand on a mouse can all signify changes in the user's emotional state, and these can all be detected and interpreted by a computer. A built-in camera captures images of the user and algorithms are used to process the data to yield meaningful information. Speech recognition and gesture recognition are among the other technologies being explored for affective computing applications [52].

Recognizing emotional information requires the extraction of meaningful patterns from the gathered data. This is done using *machine learning* techniques that process different modalities, such as speech recognition, natural language processing, or facial expression detection.

10.1 Emotion in Machines

A major area in affective computing is the design of computational devices proposed to exhibit either innate emotional capabilities or that are capable of convincingly simulating emotions. A more practical approach, based on current technological capabilities, is the simulation of emotions in conversational agents in order to enrich and facilitate interactivity between human and machine. While human emotions are often associated with surges in hormones and other neuropeptides, emotions in machines might be associated with abstract states associated with progress (or lack of progress) in autonomous learning systems. In this view, affective emotional states correspond to time-derivatives in the learning curve of an arbitrary learning system.

Two major categories describe emotions in machines: *emotional speech* and *facial affect detection* [53].

Emotional speech includes:

- Algorithms

- Databases

- Speech descriptors

Facial affect detection includes:

- Body gesture

- Physiological monitoring

10.2 The Future

Affective computing tries to address one of the major drawbacks of *online learning* versus in-classroom learning – the teacher's capability to immediately adapt the pedagogical situation to the emotional state of the student in the classroom. In *e-learning* applications, affective computing can be used to adjust the presentation style of a computerized tutor when a learner is bored, interested, frustrated, or pleased. *Psychological health services*, i.e., counseling, benefit from affective computing applications when determining a client's emotional state.

Robotic systems capable of processing affective information exhibit higher flexibility while one works in uncertain or complex environments. Companion devices, such as digital pets, use affective computing abilities to enhance realism and provide a higher degree of autonomy.

Other potential applications are centered on *social monitoring*. For example, a car can monitor the emotion of all occupants and engage in additional safety measures, such as alerting other vehicles if it detects the driver to be angry. Affective computing has potential applications in human–computer interaction, such as affective mirrors allowing the user to see how he or she performs; emotion monitoring agents sending a warning before one sends an angry email; or even music players selecting tracks based on mood. Companies would then be able to use affective computing to infer whether their products will or will not be well received by the respective market.

There are endless applications for affective computing in all aspects of life [54].

References

[51] https://en.wikipedia.org/wiki/Affective_computing
[52] http://www.gartner.com/it-glossary/affective-computing
[53] http://whatis.techtarget.com/definition/affective-computing
[54] http://curiosity.discovery.com/question/what-is-affective-computing

11

Autonomic Computing

Autonomic computing is a computer's ability to manage itself automatically through adaptive technologies that further computing capabilities and cut down on the time required by computer professionals to resolve system difficulties and other maintenance such as software updates [55].

The move toward autonomic computing is driven by a desire for cost reduction and the need to lift the obstacles presented by computer system complexities to allow for more advanced computing technology.

The autonomic computing initiative (ACI), which was developed by IBM, demonstrates and advocates networking computer systems that do not involve a lot of human intervention other than defining input rules. The ACI is derived from the autonomic nervous system of the human body.

IBM has defined the following four areas of automatic computing:

- Self-configuration

- Self-healing (error correction)

- Self-optimization (automatic resource control for optimal functioning)

- Self-protection (identification and protection from attacks in a proactive manner)

Characteristics that every autonomic computing system should have include automation, adaptivity, and awareness.

AC was designed to mimic the human body's nervous system, in that the autonomic nervous system acts and reacts to stimuli independent of the individual's conscious input – an autonomic computing environment functions with a high level of artificial intelligence while remaining invisible to the users. Just as the human body acts and responds without the individual controlling functions (e.g., internal temperature rises and falls, breathing rate fluctuates, and glands secrete hormones in response to stimulus), the autonomic computing environment operates organically in response to the input it collects [56].

IBM has set forth eight conditions that define an autonomic system:

1. The system must know itself in terms of what resources it has access to, what its capabilities and limitations are, and how and why it is connected to other systems.

2. The system must be able to automatically configure and reconfigure itself depending on the changing computing environment.

3. The system must be able to optimize its performance to ensure the most efficient computing process.

4. The system must be able to work around encountered problems by either repairing itself or routing functions away from the trouble.

5. The system must detect, identify, and protect itself against various types of attacks to maintain overall system security and integrity.

6. The system must be able to adapt to its environment as it changes, interacting with neighboring systems and establishing communication protocols.

7. The system must rely on open standards and cannot exist in a proprietary environment.

8. The system must anticipate the demand on its resources while keeping transparent to users.

Autonomic computing is one of the building blocks of *pervasive computing*, an anticipated future computing model in which tiny – even invisible – computers will be all around us, communicating through increasingly interconnected networks leading to the concept of the Internet of Everything (IoE). Many industry leaders are researching various components of autonomic computing [57].

11.1 Benefits

The main benefit of autonomic computing is reduced total cost of ownership (TCO). Breakdowns will be less frequent, thereby drastically reducing maintenance costs. Fewer personnel will be required to manage the systems. "The most immediate benefit of autonomic computing will be reduced deployment and maintenance cost , time and increased stability of IT systems through automation," says Dr. Kumar of IBM. "Higher order benefits will include allowing companies to better manage their business through IT systems that are able to adopt and implement directives based on business policy, and are able to make modifications based on changing environments." Another benefit of this technology is that it provides server consolidation to maximize system availability and minimizes cost and human effort to manage large server farms [58].

11.2 Future of Autonomic Computing

Autonomic computing promises to simplify the management of computing systems. But that capability will provide the basis for much more effective cloud computing. Other applications include server load balancing, process allocation, monitoring power supply, automatic updating of software and drivers, pre-failure warning, memory error-correction, automated system backup and recovery, etc.

References

[55] http://computer.financialexpress.com/20020819/focus1.shtml
[56] http://www.webopedia.com/TERM/A/autonomic_computing.html
[57] http://www.techopedia.com/definition/191/autonomic-computing
[58] http://whatis.techtarget.com/definition/autonomic-computing

PART 3

Big Data, Dark Data, Thick Data, and Small Data

12

Thick Data vs. Big Data

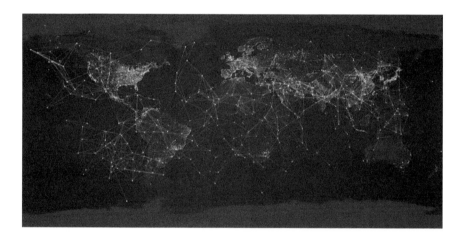

One of the challenges faced by businesses in post-COVID-19 world is the fact that consumer behavior will not go back to pre-pandemic norms. Consumers will purchase more goods and services online, and increasing numbers of people will work remotely just to mention few major changes. As companies begin to navigate the post-COVID-19 world as economies slowly begin to reopen, the use of data analytics tools will be extremely valuable in helping them adapt to these new trends. Data analytics tools will be particularly useful for detecting new purchasing patterns and delivering a greater personalized experience to customers, in addition to better understanding of consumers' new behavior [59].

However, many companies are still dealing with obstacles to successful big data projects. Across industries, the adoption of big data initiatives is way up. Spending has increased, and the vast majority of companies using big data expect return on investment. Nevertheless, companies still cite a lack of visibility into processes and information as a primary big data pain point. Modeling customer segments accurately can be impossible for businesses who do not understand why, how, and when their customers decide to make purchases for example [60].

To tackle this pain point, companies might need to consider an alternative to big data, namely thick data; it is helpful to define both terms, *big data vs. thick data* [61].

Big data is large and complex unstructured data, defined by 3 Vs. *Volume*: with big data, you will have to process high volumes of low-density, unstructured data. This can be data of unknown value, such as Facebook actions, Twitter data feeds, clickstreams on a web page or a mobile app, or sensor-enabled equipment. For some organizations, this might be tens of terabytes of data. For others, it may be hundreds of petabytes. *Velocity*: it is the fast rate at which data is received and acted on. *Variety*: it refers to the many types of data that are available. Unstructured and semi-structured data types, such as text, audio, and video, require additional preprocessing to derive meaning and support metadata.

Thick data is about a complex range of primary and secondary research approaches, including surveys, questionnaires, focus groups, interviews, journals, videos, and so on. It is the result of the collaboration between data scientists and anthropologists working together to make sense of large amounts of data. Together, they analyze data, looking for qualitative information like insights, preferences, motivations, and reasons for behaviors. At its core, thick data is qualitative data (like observations, feelings, and reactions) that provides insights into consumers' everyday emotional lives. Because thick data aims to uncover people's emotions, stories, and models of the world they live in, it can be difficult to quantify.

12.1 Comparison of Big Data and Thick Data [62]

- Big data is quantitative, while thick data is qualitative [Figure 12.1].

- Big data produces so much information that it needs something more to bridge and/or reveal knowledge gaps. Thick data uncovers the meaning behind big data visualization and analysis.

- Big data reveals insights with a particular range of data points, while thick data reveals the social context of and connections between data points.

- Big data delivers numbers; thick data delivers stories.

- Big data relies on AI/machine learning, while thick data relies on human learning.

Big Data vs. Thick Data

Figure 12.1 Big data vs. Thick data.

Thick data can be a top-notch differentiator, helping businesses uncover the kinds of insights they sometimes hope to achieve from big data alone. It can help businesses look at the big picture and put all the different stories together, while embracing the differences between each medium and using them to pull out interesting themes and contrasts. Without a counterbalance, the risk in a big data world is that organizations and individuals start making decisions and optimizing performance for metrics – metrics that are derived from algorithms, and in this whole optimization process, people, stories, actual experiences are all but forgotten.

If the big tech companies of Silicon Valley really want to "understand the world," they need to capture both its (big data) quantities and its (thick data) qualities. Unfortunately, gathering the latter requires that instead of just "seeing the world through Google Glass" (or in the case of Facebook, virtual reality), they leave the computers behind and experience the world first hand. There are two key reasons:

• To understand people, you need to understand their context.

• Most of "the world" is background knowledge.

Rather than seeking to understand us simply based on what we do as in the case of big data, thick data seeks to understand us in terms of how we relate to the many different worlds we inhabit [63].

Only by understanding our worlds can anyone really understand "the world" as a whole, which is precisely what companies like Google and

Facebook say they want to do. To "understand the world," you need to capture both its (big data) quantities and its (thick data) qualities.

In fact, companies that rely too much on the numbers, graphs, and factoids of big data risk insulating themselves from the rich, qualitative reality of their customers' everyday lives. They can lose the ability to imagine and intuit how the world – and their own businesses – might be evolving. By outsourcing our thinking to big data, our ability to make sense of the world by careful observation begins to wither, just as you miss the feel and texture of a new city by navigating it only with the help of a GPS [64, 68, 69].

Successful companies and executives work to understand the emotional, even visceral context in which people encounter their product or service, and they are able to adapt when circumstances change. They are able to use what we like to call thick data which comprises the human element of big data.

One promising technology that can give us the best of both worlds (big data and thick data) is *affective computing*.

Affective computing is the study and development of systems and devices that can recognize, interpret, process, and simulate human affects. It is an interdisciplinary field spanning computer science, psychology, and cognitive science. While the origins of the field may be traced as far back as to early philosophical enquiries into emotion ("affect" is, basically, a synonym for "emotion"), the more modern branch of computer science originated with Rosalind Picard's 1995 paper on affective computing. A motivation for the research is the ability to simulate *empathy*. The machine should interpret the emotional state of humans and adapt its behavior to them, giving an appropriate response for those emotions [65, 66, 67].

Using affective computing algorithms in gathering and processing data will make the data more human and show both sides of data: quantitative and qualitative.

References

[59] https://www.linkedin.com/pulse/8-key-tech-trends-post-covid-19-world-ahmed-banafa/

[60] https://www.bdex.com/thick-data-why-marketers-must-understand-why-people-behave-the-way-they-do/

[61] https://www.usertesting.com/blog/thick-data-vs-big-data

[62] https://www.oracle.com/in/big-data/what-is-big-data/

[63] https://www.cognizant.com/us/en/glossary/thick-data

[64] http://www.brandwatch.com/2014/04/what-is-thick-data-and-why-should-you-use-it/

[65] http://ethnographymatters.net/2013/05/13/big-data-needs-thick-data/

[66] http://www.wired.com/2014/04/your-big-data-is-worthless-if-you-dont-bring-it-into-the-real-world/

[67] http://www.big-dataforum.com/238/big-data-how-about-%E2%80%9Cthick-data%E2%80%9D-%E2%80%94-or-did-we-just-create-another-haystack

[68] http://blog.marketresearch.com/thick-data-and-market-research-understanding-your-customers

[69] http://www.wired.com/2013/03/clive-thompson-2104/

13

Understanding Dark Data

Gartner defines *dark data* as the information assets that organizations collect, process, and store during regular business activities, but generally fail to use for other purposes (for example, analytics, business relationships, and direct monetizing). Similar to dark matter in physics, dark data often comprises most organizations' universe of information assets. Thus, organizations often retain dark data for compliance purposes only. Storing and securing data typically incurs more expense (and sometimes greater risk) than value [70, 71, 73].

Dark data is a type of unstructured, untagged, and untapped data that is found in data repositories and has not been analyzed or processed. It is similar to big data but differs in how it is mostly *neglected* by business and IT administrators in terms of its value.

Dark data is also known as *dusty data*.

Dark data is data that is found in log files and data archives stored within large enterprise class data storage locations. It includes all data objects and types that have yet to be analyzed for any business or competitive intelligence or aid in business decision making. Typically, dark data is complex to analyze and store in locations where analysis is difficult. The overall process can be costly. It also can include data objects that have not been seized by the enterprise or data that are external to the organization, such as data stored by partners or customers.

IDC stated that up to 90% of big data is dark data.

With the growing accumulation of structured, unstructured, and semi-structured data in organizations – increasingly through the adoption of big data applications – dark data has come especially to denote operational data that is left unanalyzed. Such data is seen as an economic opportunity for companies if they can take advantage of it to drive new revenues or reduce internal costs. Some examples of data that is often left dark include server log files that can give clues to website visitor behavior, customer call detail records that can indicate consumer sentiment, and mobile geo-location data that can reveal traffic patterns to aid in business planning.

Dark data may also be used to describe data that can no longer be accessed because it has been stored on devices that have become obsolete [74, 75].

13.1 Types of Dark Data

1. Data that is not currently being collected.

2. Data that is being collected, but that is difficult to access at the right time and place.

3. Data that is collected and available, but that has not yet been productized, or fully applied.

Dark data, unlike dark matter, can be brought to light and so can its potential ROI. And what is more, a simple way of thinking about what to do with the data – through a cost–benefit analysis – can remove the complexity surrounding the previously mysterious dark data [77, 78].

13.2 Value of Dark Data

The primary challenge presented by dark data is not just storing it but determining its real value, if any at all. In fact, much dark data remains unilluminated because organizations simply do not know what it contains. Destroying it might be too risky, but analyzing it can be costly. And it is hard to justify that expense if the potential value of the data is unknown. To determine if their dark data is even worth further analysis, organizations need a means of quickly and cost effectively sorting, structuring, and visualizing it. An important fact in getting a handle on dark data is to understand that it is not *a one-time event*.

The first step to understand the value of dark data is identifying what information is included in your dark data, where it resides, and its current status in terms of accuracy, age, and so on. Getting to this state will require you to:

- *analyze* the data to understand the basics, such as how much you have, where it resides, and how many types (structured, unstructured, and semi-structured) are present;

- *categorize* the data to begin understanding how much of what types you have, and the general nature of information included in those types, such as format, age, etc.;

- *classify* your information according to what will happen to it next. Will it be archived? Destroyed? Studied further? Once those decisions have been made, you can send your data groups to their various homes to isolate the information that you want to explore further.

Once you have identified the relative context for your data groups, you can focus on the data you think might provide insights. You will also have a clearer picture of the full data landscape relative to your organization so that you can set information governance policies that will alleviate the burden of dark data, while also putting it to work [79].

13.3 Future of Dark Data

Startups going after dark data problems are usually not playing in existing markets with customers self-aware of their problems. They are creating new markets by surfacing new kinds of data and creating unimagined applications with that data. But when they succeed, they become big companies, ironically, with big data problems.

The question many people are asking is: what should be done with dark data? Some say data should never be thrown away, as storage is so cheap, and that data may have a purpose in the future.

References

[70] http://h30458.www3.hp.com/us/us/discover-performance/info-management-leaders/2014/jun/tapping-the-profit-potential-of-dark-data.html

[71] http://h30458.www3.hp.com/ww/en/ent/You-have-dark-data_1392257. html

[72] http://www.gartner.com/it-glossary/dark-data

[73] http://www.techopedia.com/definition/29373/dark-data

[74] http://searchdatamanagement.techtarget.com/definition/dark-data

[75] http://www.computerweekly.com/opinion/Dark-data-could-halt-big-datas-path-to-success

[76] http://www.forbes.com/sites/gartnergroup/2014/05/07/digital-business-is-everyones-business/

[77] https://medium.com/what-i-learned-building/7d88d014ba98

[78] http://blogs.pb.com/digital-insights/2014/05/05/dark-data-analytics/

[79] http://blogs.computerworld.com/business-intelligenceanalytics/23286/dark-data-when-it-worth-being-brought-light

14

Small Data vs. Big Data: Back to the Basics

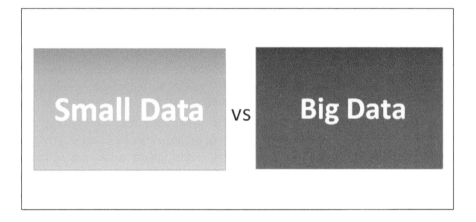

Small data is data in a volume and format that makes it accessible, informative, and actionable.

The small data group offers the following explanation:

Small data connects people with timely, meaningful insights (derived from big data and/or "local" sources), organized and packaged – often visually – to be accessible, understandable, and actionable for everyday tasks.

This definition applies to the data we have, as well as the end-user apps and analyst workbenches for turning big data sets into actionable small data. The key "action" words here are *connect*, *organize*, and *package*, and the "value" is rooted in making insights available to all (accessible), easy to apply (understandable), and focused on the task at hand (actionable) [80, 81].

The term *small data* contrasts with *big data*, which usually refers to a combination of structured and unstructured data that may be measured in petabytes or exabytes. Big data is often said to be characterized by three Vs: the volume of data, the variety of types of data, and the velocity at which it is processed, all of which combine to make big data very difficult to manage. Small data, in contrast, consists of usable chunks.

The idea of big data is compelling: want to uncover hidden patterns about customer behavior, predict the next election, or see where to focus ad spend? There is an app for that. And to listen to the pundits, we should all be telling our kids to become data scientists, since every company will need to hire an army of them to survive the next wave of digital disruption.

Yet, all the steam coming out of the big data hype machine seems to be obscuring our view of the big picture: in many cases, big data is overkill. And in most cases, big data is useful only if we (those of us who are not data scientists) can do something with it *in our everyday jobs*, which is where small data enters the picture.

At its core, the idea of small data is that businesses can get actionable results without acquiring the kinds of systems commonly used in big data analytics.

A company might invest in a whole lot of server storage and use sophisticated analytics machines and data mining applications to scour a network for lots of different bits of data, including dates and times of user actions, demographic information, and much more. All of this might get funneled into a central data warehouse, where complex algorithms sort and process the data to display it in detailed reports. While these kinds of processes have benefited businesses in a lot of ways, many enterprises are finding that these measures require a lot of effort, and that in some cases, similar results can be achieved using much less robust data mining strategies.

Small data is one of the ways that businesses are now drawing back from a kind of obsession with the latest and newest technologies that support more sophisticated business processes. Those promoting small data contend that it is important for businesses to use their resources efficiently and avoid overspending on certain types of technologies [83, 84].

14.1 Why Small Data?

- *Big data is hard*: Doing it at scale and waiting for trickle down benefits can take time. Not to mention the fact that most marketers and online strategists do not need full-on big data to target their campaigns or deliver personalized experiences.

- *Small data is all around us*: Social channels are rich with small data that is ready to be collected to inform marketing and buyer decisions. At a personal level, we are constantly *creating* this small data each time we check in, search, browse, post etc., creating a unique signature that provides a glimpse into our digital and physical health.

- *Small data is at the center of the new CRM*: Social CRM is used to create a complete picture of customers, their segments, influencers, and even competitors; we need to combine insights from social channels and campaigns with web analytics and transactional data. Small data is the key to building these rich profiles that will be the center of the new CRM solutions.

- *ROI*: A focus on the last mile of big data offers to leverage investments in small data ($10 billion and counting according to IDC) spent on upstream systems, tools, and services.

- *Data-driven marketing is the next wave*: Big (and small) data-driven marketing has the potential to revolutionize the way businesses inter-act with customers, transform how customers access and consume (and even wear) useful data, and ultimately redefine the relationship between buyers and sellers.

- *Consumer examples abound*: Consumers have seen the potential of small data to streamline their shopping, power their fitness routine, or deliver recommendations about the best price for their next flight. With more smart, wearable data-driven devices on the way, there are prom-ises to be even more market demand for packaged data and data-deliv-ery devices that "fit" the needs of everyday consumers.

- *Platform and tool vendors are starting to pay attention*: The promise of operationalizing big data and "turning insight into action" is a major tone from many of the big names in tech.

- *It is about the end-user*: Small data is about the end-user, what they need, and how they can take action. Focus on the user first, and a lot of our technology decisions become clearer.

- *Simple*: Small data is the *right data*; some small data will start life as big data, but you should not need to be a data scientist to understand or apply it for everyday tasks.

14.2 The Future of Small Data

The discussions around big data miss a much bigger and more important pic-ture: the real opportunity is not big data, but small data. Not centralized "big iron," but decentralized data wrangling. Not "one ring to rule them all" but "small pieces loosely joined."

The real revolution is the mass democratization of the means of access, storage, and processing of data; it is not about large organizations running parallel software on tens of thousands of servers, but about more people than ever being able to collaborate effectively around a distributed ecosystem of information, an ecosystem of small data.

For many problems and questions, small data in itself is enough. The data on my household energy use, the times of local buses, and government spending are all small data. Everything processed in Excel is small data. And when we want to scale up the way to do that is through componentized small data: by creating and integrating small data "packages" not building big data monoliths, by partitioning problems in a way that works across people and organizations, not through creating massive centralized silos.

This next decade belongs to distributed models not centralized ones, to collaboration not control, and to small data not big data [85, 86, 87].

References

[80] http://www.theguardian.com/news/datablog/2013/apr/25/forget-big-data-small-data-revolution
[81] http://whatis.techtarget.com/definition/small-data
[82] http://www.zdnet.com/10-reasons-2014-will-be-the-year-of-small-data-7000023667/
[83] http://www.techopedia.com/definition/29539/small-data
[84] http://technologies.lesechos.fr/partners/capgemini/cacheDirectory/HTMLcontributions/img/20120711152005_BigData.jpeg
[85] http://www.312analytics.com/wp-content/uploads/2013/03/big-data-versus-small-data1.jpg
[86] http://www.b-eye-network.com/blogs/oneal/Big%20data%20Small%20data%20v4.png
[87] https://www.rd-alliance.org/system/files/800px-BigData_SmallData.png

15

What is a Data Lake?

"*Data lake*" is a massive, easily accessible data repository for storing "*big data*." Unlike traditional data warehouses, which are optimized for data analysis by storing only some attributes and dropping data below the level aggregation, a data lake is designed to retain all attributes, especially when you do not yet know what the scope of data or its use is [88, 89, 90].

15.1 Data Lake vs. Data Warehouse

Data warehouses are large storage locations for data that you accumulate from a wide range of sources. For decades, the foundation for business intelligence and data discovery/storage rested on data warehouses. Their specific, static structures dictate what data analysis you could perform. Data warehouses are popular with mid- and large-size businesses as a way of sharing data and content across the team- or department-siloed databases. Data warehouses help organizations become more efficient. Organizations that use data

Figure 15.1 Five key components of a data lake. *Source:* dataversity.

warehouses often do so to guide management decisions – all those "data-driven" decisions you always hear about.

A *data lake* holds a vast amount of raw data in its native format until it is needed. While a hierarchical data warehouse stores data in files or folders, a data lake uses a flat architecture to store data. Each data element in a lake is assigned a unique identifier and tagged with a set of extended metadata tags. When a business question arises, the data lake can be queried for relevant data, and that smaller set of data can then be analyzed to help answer the question.

Now that data storage and technology is cheap, information is vast, and newer database technologies do not require an agreed upon schema up front, discovery analytics is finally possible. With data lakes, companies employ data scientists who are capable of making sense of untamed data as they trek through it. They can find correlations and insights within the data as they get to know it [91, 92, 93].

15.2 Five Key Components of a Data Lake Architecture

1. *Data ingestion*: A highly scalable ingestion-layer system that extracts data from various sources, such as websites, mobile apps, social media, IoT devices, and existing data management systems, is required. It should be flexible to run in batch, one-time, or real-time

modes, and it should support all types of data along with new data sources [94, 95].

2. *Data storage*: A highly scalable data storage system should be able to store and process raw data and support encryption and compression while remaining cost-effective.

3. *Data security*: Regardless of the type of data processed, data lakes should be highly secure from the use of multi-factor authentication, authorization, role-based access, data protection, etc.

4. *Data analytics*: After data is ingested, it should be quickly and efficiently analyzed using data analytics and machine learning tools to derive valuable insights and move vetted data into a data warehouse.

5. *Data governance*: The entire process of data ingestion, preparation, cataloging, integration, and query acceleration should be streamlined to produce enterprise-level data quality. It is also important to track the changes to key data elements for a data audit.

Like big data, the term *data lake* is sometimes disparaged as being simply a marketing label for a product that supports it. However, the term is being accepted as a way to describe any large data pool in which the schema and data requirements are not defined until the data is queried.

The data lake promises to speed up the delivery of information and insights to the business community without the hassles imposed by IT-centric data warehousing processes.

15.3 Data Lake Advantages [96, 97, 98]

- Data lake gives business users immediate access to *all* data

- Data in the lake is not limited to relational or transactional

- With a data lake, you never need to move the data

- Data lake empowers business users and liberating them from the bonds of IT domination

- Data lake speeds up delivery by enabling business units to stand up applications quickly

- Helps fully with product ionizing and advanced analytics

- Offers cost-effective scalability and flexibility

- Offers value from unlimited data types

- Reduces long-term cost of ownership

- Allows economic storage of files

- Quickly adaptable to changes

- The main advantage of data lake is the centralization of different content sources

- Users, from various departments, may be scattered around the globe and can have flexible access to the data

15.4 Data Lake Disadvantages

- Unknown area of data processing

- Data governance

- Dealing with chaos

- Privacy issues

- Complexity of legacy data

- Metadata lifecycle management

- Desolate data islands

- The issue of integration

- Unstructured data may lead to ungoverned and unusable data, and disparate and complex tools

- Increases storage and computes costs

- There is no way to get insights from others who have worked with the data because there is no account of the lineage of findings by previous analysts

- The biggest risk of data lakes is security and access control. Some data can be placed into a lake without any oversight, as some of the data may have privacy and regulatory need [99, 100, 101]

15.5 The Future

There are many organizations that are making this approach a reality; the internal infrastructures developed at Google, Amazon, and Facebook provide their developers with the advantages and agility of the data lake dream. For each of these companies, the data lake created a value chain through which new types of business value emerged:

- Using data lakes for web data increased the speed and quality of web search.

- Using data lakes for clickstream data supported more effective methods of web advertising.

- Using data lakes for cross-channel analysis of customer interactions and behaviors provided a more complete view of the customer.

- Data lakes can give retailers profitable insights from raw data, such as log files, streaming audio and video, text files, and social media content, among other sources, to quickly identify real-time consumer behavior and convert actions into sales. Such 360° profile views allow stores to better interact with customers and push on-the-spot, customized offers to retain business or acquire new sales.

- Data lakes can help companies improve their R&D performance by allowing researchers to make more informed decisions regarding the wealth of highly complex data assets that feed advanced predictive and prescriptive analytics.

- Companies can use data lakes to centralize disparate data generated from a variety of sources and run analytics and ML algorithms to be the first to identify business opportunities. For instance, a biotechnology company can implement a data lake that receives manufacturing data, research data, customer support data, and public data sets and provide real-time visibility into the research process for various user communities via different user interfaces.

Regardless of where you are now, take some time to look to the future. We are on a journey toward connecting enterprise data together. As business is increasingly becoming pure digital, access to data will become a critical priority, as will speed of development and deployment. The data lake is a dream that can match those demands. The global data lake market was valued at $7.9 billion in 2019 and is expected to grow at a compound annual growth rate (CAGR) of 20.6% by 2024 to reach $20.1 billion [102, 103].

References

[88] https://www.bmc.com/blogs/data-lake-vs-data-warehouse-vs-database-whats-the-difference/

[89] https://www.guru99.com/data-lake-architecture.html#21

[90] https://www.dataversity.net/data-lakes-what-they-are-and-how-to-use-them/

[91] http://www.gartner.com/newsroom/id/2809117?

[92] http://datascience101.wordpress.com/2014/03/12/what-is-a-data-lake/

[93] http://en.wiktionary.org/wiki/data_lake

[94] http://searchaws.techtarget.com/definition/data-lake

[95] http://www.forbes.com/sites/edddumbill/2014/01/14/the-data-lake-dream/

[96] http://www.platfora.com/wp-content/uploads/2014/06/data-lake.png

[97] http://www.b-eye-network.com/blogs/eckerson/archives/2014/03/beware_of_the_a.php

[98] http://usblogs.pwc.com/emerging-technology/the-future-of-big-data-data-lakes/

[99] http://siliconangle.com/blog/2014/08/07/gartner-drowns-the-concept-of-data-lakes-in-new-report/

[100] http://www.pwc.com/us/en/technology-forecast/2014/issue1/features/data-lakes.jhtml

[101] http://www.ibmbigdatahub.com/blog/don%E2%80%99t-drown-big-data-lake http://www.wallstreetandtech.com/data-management/what-is-a-data-lake/d/d-id/1268851?

[102] http://emcplus.typepad.com/.a/6a0168e71ada4c970c01a3fc-c11630970b-800wi

[103] http://hortonworks.com/wp-content/uploads/2014/05/TeradataHortonworks_Datalake_White-Paper_20140410.pdf

PART 4

Cloud Computing

16

Edge Computing Paradigm

Edge computing is a model in which data, processing, and applications are concentrated in devices at the network rather than existing almost entirely in the cloud.

Edge computing is a paradigm that extends cloud computing and services to the network; similar to cloud, edge provides data, computation, storage, and application services to end-users [See Figure 16.1].

Edge computing reduces service latency and improves quality of service (QoS), resulting in superior user-experience. Edge computing supports emerging concept of metaverse applications that demand real-time/predictable latency (industrial automation, transportation, and networks of sensors and actuators). Edge computing paradigm is well positioned for real time big data and real-time analytics; it supports densely distributed data collection points, hence adding a fourth axis to the often-mentioned big data dimensions (volume, variety, and velocity) [104, 105].

Unlike traditional data centers, edge devices are geographically distributed over heterogeneous platforms, spanning multiple management domains. That means data can be processed locally in smart devices rather than being sent to the cloud for processing.

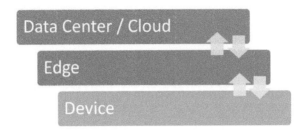

Figure 16.1   Edge computing.

Edge computing services cover the following:

• Applications that require very low and predictable latency

• Geographically distributed applications

• Fast mobile applications

• Large-scale distributed control systems

16.1 Advantages of Edge Computing [Figure 16.2]

• *Bringing data close to the user.* Instead of housing information at data center sites far from the end-point, the edge aims to place the data close to the end-user.

• *Creating dense geographical distribution.* First of all, big data and analytics can be done faster with better results. Second, administrators are able to support location-based mobility demands and not have to traverse the entire network. Third, these (edge) systems would be created in such a way that real-time data analytics become a reality on a truly massive scale.

• *True support for mobility and the metaverse.* By controlling data at various points, edge computing integrates core cloud services with those of a truly distributed data center platform. As more services are created to benefit the end-user, an edge network will become more prevalent.

• *Numerous verticals are ready to adopt.* Many organizations are already adopting the concept of the edge. Many different types of services aim to deliver rich content to the end-user. This spans IT shops, vendors, and entertainment companies as well.

• *Seamless integration with the cloud and other services.* With edge services, we are able to enhance the cloud experience by isolating user

Figure 16.2 Benefits of edge computing.

data that needs to live on the edge. From there, administrators are able to tie-in analytics, security, or other services directly into their cloud model.

16.2 Benefits of Edge Computing

- Minimize latency

- Conserve network bandwidth

- Address security concerns at all levels of the network

- Operate reliably with quick decisions

- Collect and secure wide range of data

- Move data to the best place for processing

- Lower expenses of using high computing power only when needed and less bandwidth

- Better analysis and insights of local data

16.3 Real-Life Example

A traffic light system in a major city is equipped with smart sensors. It is the day after the local team won a championship game and it is the morning of the day of the big parade. A surge of traffic into the city is expected as revelers come to celebrate their team's win. As the traffic builds, data are collected from individual traffic lights. The application developed by the city to adjust light patterns and timing is running on each edge device. The app automatically makes adjustments to light patterns in real time, at the edge, working around traffic impediments as they arise and diminish. Traffic delays are kept to a minimum, and fans spend less time in their cars and have more time to enjoy their big day [106].

After the parade is over, all the data collected from the traffic light system would be sent up to the cloud and analyzed, supporting predictive analysis and allowing the city to adjust and improve its traffic application's response to future traffic anomalies. There is little value in sending a live steady stream of everyday traffic sensor data to the cloud for storage and analysis. The civic engineers have a good handle on normal traffic patterns. The relevant data is sensor information that diverges from the norm, such as the data from parade day.

16.4 Future of Edge Computing

As more services, data, and applications are pushed to the end-user, technologists will need to find ways to optimize the *delivery process*. This means bringing information closer to the end-user, reducing latency and being prepared for the metaverse and its applications in Web 3.0. More users are utilizing mobility as their means to conduct business and their personal lives. Rich content and lots of data points are pushing cloud computing platforms, literally, to the edge – where the user's requirements are continuing to grow.

With the increase in data and cloud services utilization, edge computing will play a key role in helping reduce latency and improving the user experience. We are now truly distributing the data plane and pushing advanced services to the edge. By doing so, administrators are able to bring rich content to the user faster, more efficiently, and – very importantly – more economically. This, ultimately, will mean better data access, improved corporate analytics capabilities, and an overall improvement in the end-user computing experience.

Moving the intelligent processing of data to the edge only raises the stakes for maintaining the availability of these smart gateways and their communication path to the cloud. When the Internet of Things (IoT) provides methods that allow people to manage their daily lives, from locking their homes to checking their schedules to cooking their meals, gateway downtime in the edge computing world becomes a critical issue. Additionally, resilience and failover solutions that safeguard those processes will become even more essential. Generally speaking, we are moving toward localization to distributed model away from the current strained centralized system defining the internet infrastructure [107, 108].

References

[104] https://www.linkedin.com/pulse/why-iot-needs-fog-computing-ahmed-banafa/
[105] https://www.linkedin.com/pulse/fog-computing-vital-successful-internet-things-iot-ahmed-banafa/
[106] http://www.cisco.com/web/about/ac50/ac207/crc_new/university/RFP/rfp13078.html
[107] http://www.howtogeek.com/185876/what-is-Edge-computing/
[108] http://newsroom.cisco.com/feature-content?type=webcontent&-articleId=1365576

17

The Internet of Everything

The Internet of Everything was listed as one of the top tech trends. The term Internet of Everything (IoE) is a fairly new term, and there is a confusion about the difference between the Internet of Everything (IoE) and the Internet of Things (IoT); to clarify that, let us start with definitions and applications and explore the future of this new concept [109, 110].

17.1 What is the Internet of Everything (IoE)?

The Internet of Everything (IoE) "is bringing together people, process, data, and things to make networked connections more relevant and valuable than ever before-turning information into actions that create new capabilities, richer experiences, and unprecedented economic opportunity for businesses, individuals, and countries".

In simple terms, IoE is the intelligent connection of people, process, data, and things. The Internet of Everything (IoE) describes a world where billions of objects have sensors to detect, measure, and assess their status; all are connected over public or private networks using standard and proprietary protocols [112, 118].

17.2 Pillars of the Internet of Everything (IoE)

- *People*: Connecting people in more relevant, valuable ways

- *Data:* Converting data into intelligence to make better decisions

- *Process:* Delivering the right information to the right person (or machine) at the right time

- *Things:* Physical devices and objects connected to the internet and each other for intelligent decision making; it is often called *Internet of Things (IoT)*

17.3 The Internet of Things (IoT)

The Internet of Things (IoT) is the network of physical objects accessed through the internet. These objects contain embedded technology to interact with internal states or the external environment. In other words, when objects can sense and communicate, it changes how and where decisions are made, and who makes them; for example, Nest thermostats [113].

17.4 The Difference Between IoE and IoT

The Internet of Everything (IoE) with four pillars, people, process, data, and things, builds on top of the Internet of Things (IoT) with one pillar, things. In addition, IoE further advances the power of the internet to improve business and industry outcomes and ultimately make people's lives better by adding to the progress of IoT (*Dave Evans, Chief Futurist Cisco Consulting Services) [114].*

17.5 The Future

The Internet of Everything will re-invent industries at three levels*: business process*, *business model*, and *business moment.*

"At the first level, digital technology is improving our products, services and *processes*, our customer and constituent experiences, and the way we work in our organizations and within our partnerships," said Hung Le Hong, research vice president and Gartner Fellow. "We do what we normally do, but digitalization allows us to do it better or develop better products within our industry."

As companies digitalize products and processes, completely new ways of doing business in industries emerge. Gartner analysts expect more transformational changes as digitalization re-invents industries at the business *model* level. Mr. Le Hong gave the examples of Nike, playing on the edge of the healthcare industry with its connected sporting clothes and gear, and Google having a visible presence in autonomous vehicles. "These organizations had no business in your industry, and are now re-inventing them," said Mr. Le Hong [115].

The third level of digital re-invention is created by the need to compete with unprecedented business velocity and agility. Gartner calls this the *"business moment."*

The Internet of Everything will create tens of millions of new objects and sensors, all generating real-time data. *"Data is money,"* said Nick Jones, research vice president and distinguished analyst at Gartner. "Businesses will need *big data* and *storage technologies* to collect, analyze and store the sheer volume of information. Furthermore, to turn data into money business and IT leaders will need decisions. As they won't have the time or the capacity to make all the decisions themselves they will need processing power."

"Now that digital is embedded in everything we do, every business needs its own flavor of digital strategy. Vanilla is off the menu," said Dave Aron, research vice president and Gartner Fellow. "Digital is not an option, not an add-on, and not an afterthought; it is the new reality that requires a comprehensive digital leadership."

Gartner predicts that enterprises will make extensive use of IoE technology, and there will be a wide range of products sold into various markets. These will include advanced medical devices, factory automation sensors and applications in industrial robotics, sensor motes for increased agricultural yield, and automotive sensors and infrastructure integrity monitoring systems for diverse areas such as road and railway transportation, water distribution, and electrical transmission; an endless list of products and services.

But as devices get more connected and collect more data, *privacy* and *security* concerns will increase too. How companies decide to balance customer privacy with this wealth of IoE data will be critical [117].

References

[109] http://www.cisco.com/web/about/ac79/innov/IoE.html
[110] http://internetofeverything.cisco.com/
[111] http://www.cisco.com/web/solutions/trends/iot/overview.html
[112] http://time.com/#539/the-next-big-thing-for-tech-the-internet-of-everything/
[113] http://www.gartner.com/newsroom/id/2621015

[114] http://www.livemint.com/Specials/34DC3bDLSCItBaTfRvMBQO/
        Internet-of-Everything-gains-momentum.html
[115] http://www.tibco.com/blog/2013/10/07/gartners-internet-of-everything/
[116] http://www.eweek.com/small-business/internet-of-everything-personal-
        worlds-creating-new-markets-gartner.html
[117] "Secure and Smart IoT" Book, Ahmed Banafa
[118] https://www.linkedin.com/pulse/20140319132744-246665791-the-
        internet-of-everything-ioe/

18

Content Delivery Networks – CDNs

A *content delivery network* or *content distribution network* (*CDN*) is a large distributed system of servers deployed in multiple data centers across the internet. The goal of a CDN is to serve content to end-users with high availability and high performance. CDNs serve a large fraction of the internet content today, including web objects (text, graphics, and scripts), downloadable objects (media files, software, and documents), applications (e-commerce and portals), live streaming media, on-demand streaming media, and social networks [119].

18.1 Dynamics of CDNs

A CDN is a system of distributed servers (network) that deliver webpages and other web content to a user based on the geographic *locations* of the user, the *origin* of the webpage, and a *content* delivery server. This service is effective in speeding the delivery of content of websites with high traffic and websites that have global reach. The closer the CDN server is to the user geographically, the faster the content will be delivered to the user. CDNs also provide protection from large surges in traffic [120].

Servers nearest to the website visitor respond to the request. The CDN copies the pages of a website to a network of servers that are dispersed at geographically different locations, caching the contents of the page. When a user requests a webpage that is part of a content delivery network, the CDN will redirect the request from the originating site's server to a server in the CDN that is closest to the user and deliver the cached content. The CDN will also communicate with the originating server to deliver any content that has not been previously cached. The process of bouncing through a CDN is nearly *transparent* to the user.

In a CDN, content exists in multiple copies on strategically dispersed servers. This is known as *content replication*. A large CDN can have thousands of servers, making it possible to provide identical content to many users efficiently and reliably even at times of maximum Internet traffic or during sudden demand "spikes." When a specific page, file, or program is requested by a user, the server closest to that user (*in terms of the minimum number of **nodes** between the server and the user*) is dynamically determined. This optimizes the speed with which the content is delivered to that user [121, 122].

18.2 Difference Between Serving Content without a CDN and with a CDN

The use of CDN technology has obvious economic advantages to enterprises who expect, or experience, large numbers of hits on their web sites from locations all over the world. If dozens or hundreds of other users happen to select the same web page or content simultaneously, the CDN sends the content to each of them without delay or time-out. Problems with excessive latency, as well as large variations in latency from moment to moment (which can cause annoying "jitter" in streaming audio and video), are minimized. The bandwidth each user "sees" is maximized. The difference is noticed most by users with high-speed internet connections who often demand streaming content or large files.

Another advantage of CDN technology is content redundancy that provides a fail-safe feature and allows for graceful degradation in the event of damage to, or malfunction of, a part of the internet. Even during a large-scale attack that disables many servers, content on a CDN will remain available to at least some users. Still another advantage of CDN technology is the fact that it inherently offers enhanced data backup, archiving, and storage capacity. This can benefit individuals and enterprises that rely on online data backup.

A complete CDN architecture is made up of various individual components working toward the common goal of delivering service to the end-user community. A common example of a CDN can be a consolidated file server that is used as the user application and data file warehouse. The common functions associated with the content delivery network include *file accessibility*, *application processing*, *multimedia delivery*, and *caching*. A complete CDN has the ability to exhibit functionalities that are only possible because of the participation of each separate CDN component.

The strategically placed servers have a higher capacity compared to a network backbone, which maximizes the potential to increase the number of simultaneous users. In addition, such strategically placed edge servers lower the delivery time and decrease load on public and private peers, backbones, and interconnects. A CDN manages the full load of traffic by readdressing it toward the *edge servers* [123].

Figure 18.1 CDN types of services.

18.3 Types of Services

- *Web acceleration*: A CDN may augment acceleration via compression between nodes in its own network. Quite often, only the graphics on a web page are delivered by the CDN, while the HTML text is sent out from the customer's servers.

- *Streaming and downloading*: Video uses extensive network bandwidth, and many customers of a CDN use the service solely to stream video to web users. A CDN may offer all popular streaming methods such as Flash, Windows Media, Silverlight, and progressive download.

- *Server-side processing*: The CDN may offer server-side processing of Java and ASP scripts.

- *Hybrid CDN (peer-to-peer)*: A CDN may support peer-to-peer processing, which requires client software to be installed in the user's computer or pre-installed in a set-top box.

- *Search engine optimization (SEO)*: Search engines now penalize sites that load too slowly, and broadband penetration has created unprecedented traffic jams. Fast connection times do little good for viewers if the content delivers slowly.

- *Redundancy for fail-safe*: CDN technology provides redundancy for fail-safe protection during partial internet malfunctions. Duplication of content also protects against loss of data and image degradation.

18.4 Advantages of CDNs

- Eliminate pauses and accommodate heavy traffic

- Minimize packet loss

- Faster loading

- File mirroring

- Optimize live delivery

- Enable linear networks

- Support video on demand

- Scalability

18.5 Disadvantages of CDNs

- New points of failure

- Sharing resources

- Geographical choice considerations

- Content management problems

- Lack of direct control

- Costs

18.6 The Future

Studies suggest that web *video delivery* (streaming) will see some of the biggest growth, and the popularity of *mobile apps* helps to illustrate how the CDN of tomorrow might look. The explosive growth of subscribers in streaming services for movies and shows supports this prediction, especially after a year of WFH, in addition to the non-stop use of videoconferencing services for live meetings.

As more and more people access the internet on mobile devices, delivering data across low bandwidth, high latency networks are likely to be the main battleground for those developing high performance data acceleration technologies. Add to this the increasing popularity of cloud-based services, such as online software as service applications and cloud storage, and you can begin to get an idea of how CDN providers will tackle the issue of poor performance in years to come. In addition to that, the introduction of 5G networks will open another avenue for such delivery and lower the stress on other traditional networks. Deployment of Wi-Fi 6 is also another promising technology to help in this mix, and 10 years from now, we will see 6G with astronomical speed of delivery, which will change the landscape of CDNs.

Whilst it seems that the short-term future of the content delivery network is assured, the world of online data is constantly evolving. As new technologies create support for increasingly complex types of files, it is more important than ever for CDN providers to invest in new technologies to ensure that they can meet the demand that will be generated over the coming years [124].

References

[119] http://www.webopedia.com/TERM/C/CDN.html

[120] http://searchaws.techtarget.com/definition/content-delivery-network-CDN

[121] http://en.wikipedia.org/wiki/Content_delivery_network

[122] http://www.akamai.com/html/solutions/sola_cdn.html

[123] http://www.techopedia.com/definition/4191/content-delivery-network-cdn

[124] http://www.pcmag.com/encyclopedia/term/39466/cdn

19

Network Functions Virtualization (NFV) or Software-Defined Networking (SDN)?

19.1 What is Network Functions Virtualization (NFV)?

Network functions virtualization (NFV) is a network architecture concept that proposes using IT virtualization related technologies, to virtualize entire classes of network node functions into building blocks that may be connected, or chained, together to create communication services.

Network functions virtualization (NFV) offers a new way to design, deploy, and manage networking services. NFV decouples the network functions, such as network address translation (NAT), firewalling, intrusion detection, domain name service (DNS), caching, etc., from proprietary hardware appliances; so they can run in software.

It is designed to consolidate and deliver the networking components needed to support a fully virtualized infrastructure – including virtual servers,

97

storage, and even other networks. It utilizes standard IT virtualization technologies that run on high-volume service, switch and storage hardware to virtualize network functions. It is applicable to any data plane processing or control plane function in both wired and wireless network infrastructures [125].

19.2 The Benefits of NFV [126]

- *Reduce CapEx*: Reducing the need to purchase purpose-built hardware and supporting pay-as-you-grow models to eliminate wasteful overprovisioning.

- *Reduce OpEX:* Reducing space, power, and cooling requirements of equipment and simplifying the roll-out and management of network services.

- *Accelerate time-to-market*: Reducing the time to deploy new networking services to support changing business requirements, seize new market opportunities, and improve return on investment of new services.

- *Deliver agility and flexibility*: Quickly scale up or down services to address changing demands; support innovation by enabling services to be delivered via software on any industry-standard server hardware.

- *Enable innovation:* Enabling organizations to create new types of applications, services, and business models.

19.3 Types of NFV [127]

Almost *any network function* can be virtualized. The NFV focus in the market today includes the following:

- *Virtual switching*: Physical ports are connected to virtual ports on virtual servers with virtual routers using virtualized IPsec and SSL VPN gateways.

- *Virtualized network appliances*: Network functions that today require a dedicated box can be replaced with a virtual appliance. Examples include firewalls, web security, IPS/IDS, WAN acceleration, and optimization.

- *Virtualized network services*: Examples here are network management applications such as traffic analysis, network monitoring tools, load balancers, and accelerators.

- *Virtualized applications*: Almost any application you can imagine. For example, there is a great deal of development today for cloud applications, such as virtualized storage and photo imaging services, to support the explosion in tablet and smartphone usage.

19.4 Which is Better – SDN or NFV?

Whereas SDN was created by researchers and data center architects, NFV was created by a consortium of service providers. Software-defined networking (SDN) and network functions virtualization (NFV) are all complementary approaches. They each offer a new way to design, deploy, and manage the network and its services [128].

- *SDN:* Separates the network's control (brains) and forwarding (muscle) planes and provides a centralized view of the distributed network for more efficient orchestration and automation of network services.

- *NFV:* Focuses on optimizing the network services themselves. NFV decouples the network functions, such as DNS, caching, etc., from proprietary hardware appliances; so they can run in software to accelerate service innovation and provisioning, particularly within service provider environments.

SDN and NFV each aim to advance a *software-based approach* to networking for more *scalable*, *agile*, and *innovative* networks that can better align and support the overall IT objectives of the business. It is not surprising that some common doctrines guide the development of each.

They each aim to:

- Move functionality to software

- Use commodity servers and switches over proprietary appliances

- Leverage programmatic application interfaces (APIs)

- Support more efficient orchestration, virtualization, and automation of network services

These approaches are *mutually beneficial* but are not dependent on one another. You do not need one to have the other. However, the reality is SDN makes NFV more compelling and vice-versa. SDN contributes network automation that enables policy-based decisions to orchestrate which network traffic goes where, while NFV focuses on the services it is supporting. The advancement of all these technologies is the key to evolving the network to keep pace with the innovations of all the people and devices it is connecting [129].

19.5 The Future of NFV

NFV could also be extended to non-connectivity features of the network. Probably, the most relevant of these use cases is *context-aware networking* or the ability to make performance and provisioning decisions based on location, user activity, and even social context. If users are busy, they do not have to receive application access. Or they can receive varying levels of access depending on the type of application they need.

NFV is about function hosting, and there are many ways to host functions – from appliances to dedicated servers, through virtualization and via the cloud. But NFV will create a framework for deploying complex applications and operating them with high reliability and low operational expenditure costs. This will allow operators to price even complex contextual applications at levels that are consistent with broad adoption and still make a satisfactory profit from their investment. It will also allow operators to bring new services to market faster, accelerating revenue realization and encouraging investment [130].

References

[125] http://www.6wind.com/software-defined-networking/sdn-nfv-primer/
[126] http://www.tmcnet.com/tmc/whitepapers/documents/whitepapers/
         2013/9377-network-functions-virtualization-challenges-solutions.pdf
[127] http://www.sdncentral.com/why-sdn-software-defined-networking-
         or-nfv-network-functions-virtualization-now/
[128] http://www.sdncentral.com/technology/nfv-and-sdn-whats-the-
         difference/2013/03/
[129] http://www.sdncentral.com/whats-network-functions-virtualization-nfv/
[130] http://www.sdncentral.com/which-is-better-sdn-or-nfv/

20

What is Virtualization?

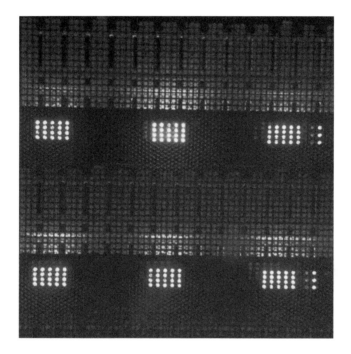

20.1 What is Virtualization?

Virtualization is software that separates physical infrastructures to create various dedicated resources. It is the fundamental technology that powers *cloud computing*.

"Virtualization software makes it possible to run multiple operating systems and multiple applications on the same server at the same time," said Mike Adams, director of product marketing at VMware. "It enables businesses to reduce IT costs while increasing the efficiency, utilization and flexibility of their existing computer hardware [131]."

20.2 Types of Virtualizations

- *Network virtualization* is a method of combining the available resources in a network by splitting up the available bandwidth into channels, each of which is independent from the others, and each of which can be assigned (or reassigned) to a particular server or device in real time. The idea is that virtualization disguises the true complexity of the network by separating it into manageable parts; much like your partitioned hard drive makes it easier to manage your files.

- *Storage virtualization* is the pooling of physical storage from multiple network storage devices into what appears to be a single storage device that is managed from a central console. Storage virtualization is commonly used in storage area networks (SANs).

- *Server virtualization* is the masking of server resources (including the number and identity of individual physical servers, processors, and operating systems) from server users. The intention is to spare the user from having to understand and manage complicated details of server resources while increasing resource sharing and utilization and maintaining the capacity to expand later.

- *Desktop virtualization*: Deploying desktops as a managed service gives you the opportunity to respond quicker to changing needs and opportunities. You can reduce costs and increase service by quickly and easily delivering virtualized desktops and applications to branch offices, outsourced and offshore employees, and mobile workers on iPad and Android tablets.

- *Application virtualization*: Organizations are increasingly virtualizing more of their Tier 1 mission-critical business applications and platforms, such as databases, ERP, CRM, email, collaboration, Java middleware, business intelligence, and many others [132].

Virtualization provides the following benefits:

- Cost saving

- Efficiently using hardware, virtualization can reduce the number of physical systems you need to acquire, and you can get more value out of the servers

- Runs multiple types of applications and operating systems on the same physical hardware

- Ease of application deployment

- IT budget integration [133]

20.3 How is Virtualization Different from Cloud Computing?

Cloud computing and virtualization are two approaches to computing that attempt to make more efficient use of computer hardware. *Cloud computing* is a form of internet-based computing that delivers resources such as storage space and processing time on a pay-per-use basis. *Virtualization* creates simulated resources and allows a single piece of hardware to deliver multiple services at once. Both options can save money by using computer hardware more efficiently. The primary difference between the two is that the physical resources that power cloud computing are owned by a cloud service provider, while a corporation that uses virtualization still maintains servers and computer hardware in its own data centers.

20.4 The Future of Virtualization

Virtualization has enabled the cloud, but how will it shape it in the future?

Cloud computing and virtualization go hand in hand. Virtualization is cloud's foundation and cloud computing software. But as the cloud evolves, so too must virtualization to support more IO-intensive network and storage workloads, and to ensure that open standards being developed across the industry can also be applied to *hypervisor* (virtual machine manager) designs. Most clouds today run on virtualization technology that is 10 years old. But work is taking place behind the scenes to revolutionize the way virtualization is done [134, 135].

References

[131] http://www.businessnewsdaily.com/5791-virtualization-vs-cloud-computing.html
[132] http://searchservervirtualization.techtarget.com/definition/virtualization
[133] http://www.vmware.com/virtualization
[134] http://www.wisegeek.com/what-are-the-benefits-of-virtualization.htm
[135] http://www.datacenterdynamics.com/focus/archive/2013/10/future-virtualization

21

Risks of Cloud Computing Explained (Both Sides)

Cloud computing continues to transform the way organizations are doing business, proving to be a transformative innovation for many enterprises. It allows employees to work virtually so that they can access company files from anywhere they can acquire an internet connection; it allows businesses to streamline their operations and develop more eco-friendly strategies, and cloud-based systems have consistently proven to be more reliable and cost-efficient than in-house infrastructures [136].

In 2020, cloud computing reached a $300 billion industry, and for good reason – whether users are on a desktop computer or mobile device, the cloud provides instant access to data anytime, anywhere there is an internet connection. For businesses, cloud computing also offers myriad benefits, such as scalable storage for files, applications, and other types of data; improved collaboration regardless of team members' locations; and saved time and money by eliminating the need to build a costly data center and hire an IT team to manage it.

Most businesses, however, have one major concern when it comes to cloud computing: Exactly how safe is the cloud? Although most reputable cloud providers have top-of-the-line security to protect users' data, experts say that there is no such thing as a completely safe cloud system.

Considering how far the cloud has come in recent years spurs questions of what kind of risks are faced by businesses when using cloud computing, the following list can help.

From the perspective of the providers:

- *Security and privacy*: Data integration and ownership concerns persist. These concerns need to be addressed for the protection of intellectual property, employee, customer, and partner information.

- *Governance*: Without oversight, business leaders will be able to create shadow IT components or entire organizations. And within IT, there are fewer barriers to creating unapproved environments.

- *Competition*: Enables start-ups to avoid most of the hazards of building a technology foundation accelerating the rise from start-up to stalwart.

- *Regulatory*: Ensuring compliance with the myriad of rules including SOX, HIPAA, PCI, and others while taking advantage of the economic model.

- *Bandwidth*: Network bandwidth is the most important component of the model without which the model is an illiquid asset.

- *Staff*: Cloud expertise will be difficult to keep as more companies jump on the bandwagon and want to profit from the price paid by early adopters [137].

From the perspective of the customers:

- *Multi-tenancy (shared access)*: The problem with shared access is that there is a risk that your company's sensitive data could accidentally show up in someone else's space.

- *Network availability*: When you work from the cloud, you are at the mercy of its availability. This means that if your provider's systems go down, so does your access and productivity.

- *Ownership of data*: Before you upload any files to the cloud, double check your contract to make sure your property remains your property.

- *Data integrity*: If you think that your data security is questionable when you store it on-site, imagine the risk when your data is being stored at a location you do not even know.

- *Virtualization*: Practically every cloud service provider uses virtualization. As a result, users do not only have to worry about the risks associated with physical machines but also with the unique risks associated with virtual server hosts and the guests that access them.

- *Authentication, authorization, and access control*: Your cloud vendor's choice of authentication, authorization, and access control mechanisms is crucial, but a lot depends on process as well.

- *Cyberattacks*: Any time you store data on the internet, you are at the risk for a cyberattack. This is particularly problematic on the cloud, where volumes of data are stored by all types of users on the same cloud system.

- *Insider threats*: Just as cyberattacks are on the rise, so are security breaches from the inside. Once an employee gains or gives others access to your cloud, everything from customer data to confidential information and intellectual property are up for grabs.

- *Government intrusion*: With the recent NSA leaks and the ensuing reports on government surveillance programs, competitors are not the only ones who may want to take a peek at your data.

- *Legal liability*: Risks associated with the cloud are not limited to security breaches. They also include its aftermath, such as lawsuits filed by or against you. "The latest risks to using cloud for business are compliance, legal liability and business continuity," said Robert J. Scott, managing partner of *Scott & Scott LLP*, an intellectual property and technology law firm. "Data breach incidences are on the rise, and so are lawsuits."

- *Lack of standardization*: A provider could have the latest security features, but due to the general lack of cloud standardization, there are no clear-cut guidelines unifying cloud providers [138].

21.1 The Risks Will Never Diminish

The biggest risk when it comes to cloud computing is that you never know what is up ahead. Hackers have been around from the start and they are not going anywhere any time soon. And as technology advances, so do the risks that come with adopting them.

For business using or considering migrating to the cloud, all you can do is be as prepared as you can possibly be. The key is getting to know providers as much as you can, both as a company and from an end-user perspective [139, 140].

References

[136] http://www.businessnewsdaily.com/5215-dangers-cloud-computing.html
[137] http://www.liquidtechnology.net/blog/cloud-computing-security-risks/
[138] http://www.pwc.com/us/en/issues/cloud-computing/risks.jhtml
[139] http://www.networkworld.com/article/2226230/cisco-subnet/security-professionals-identify-it-risks-associated-with-cloud-computing.html
[140] http://www.infoworld.com/d/security/the-5-cloud-risks-you-have-stop-ignoring-214696?page=0,1

22

Cloud-of-Clouds or (Intercloud)

Intercloud or *"cloud-of-clouds"* is a term that refers to a theoretical model for cloud computing services based on the idea of combining many different individual clouds into one seamless mass in terms of on-demand operations. The intercloud would simply make sure that a cloud could use resources beyond its reach, by taking advantage of pre-existing contracts with other cloud providers [141].

The intercloud scenario is based on the key concept that each single cloud does not have infinite physical resources or ubiquitous geographic footprint. If a cloud saturates the computational and storage resources of its infrastructure or is requested to use resources in a geography where it has no footprint, it would still be able to satisfy such requests for service allocations sent from its clients.

The intercloud scenario would address such situations where each cloud would use the computational storage or any kind of resource (through semantic resource descriptions, and open federation) of the infrastructures of other clouds. This is analogous to the way the internet works, in that a service provider, to which an endpoint is attached, will access or deliver traffic from/to source/destination addresses outside of its service area by using internet routing protocols with other service providers with whom it has a pre-arranged exchange or peering relationship. It is also analogous to the way mobile operators implement roaming and inter-carrier interoperability. Such forms of cloud exchange, peering, or roaming may introduce new business opportunities among cloud providers if they manage to go beyond the theoretical framework [142].

IBM researchers are working on a solution that they claim can seamlessly store and move data across multiple cloud platforms in real time. The firm thinks that the technology will help enterprises with service reliability concerns. On top of this, they hope to "cloud-enable" almost any digital storage product.

Researchers at IBM have developed a "drag-and-drop" toolkit that allows users to move file storage across almost any cloud platform. The company cloud would host identity authentication and encryption technologies as well as other security systems on an external cloud platform (the "InterCloud Store") to keep each cloud autonomous, while also keeping them synced together.

IBM's Evangelos Eleftheriou explained that the cloud-of-clouds invention can help avoid service outrages due to the fact that it can tolerate crashes of any number of clients. It would do this by using the independence of multiple clouds linked together to increase the overall reliability.

Storage services do not communicate directly with each other but instead go through the larger cloud for authentication. Data is encrypted as it leaves one station and decrypted before it reaches the next. If one cloud happens to fail, a back-up cloud responds immediately.

The cloud-of-clouds is also intrinsically more secure: "If one provider gets hacked there is little chance they will penetrate other systems at the same time using the same vulnerability," says Alessandro Sorniotti, cloud storage scientist at IBM and one of the researchers. "From the client perspective, we will have the most available and secure storage system."

HP and RedHat have also made offerings of similar kinds, Cisco will invest $1B in the next two years to build its expanded cloud business, and we expect the incremental capabilities to expand the true investment figure even further [143].

22.1 The Future

Five years from now, there will be a suite of international interoperability standards that will lead to a cloud-of-clouds, or "intercloud," a future where there will be tight integration between multiple clouds. This tighter integration of clouds will have practical implications for businesses, giving analysts the ability to sift through silos of big data applications to make better informed decisions, according to John Messina, a senior member with the National Institute of Standards and Technology's cloud computing program. "Interoperability is much broader than an organization or consumers talking with cloud providers, but also involves cloud providers communicating with one another and those providers interconnecting with other resources such as social media and sensor networks," Messina said [144].

NIST along with other international groups such as the Institute of Electrical and Electronics Engineers, the International Electrotechnical Commission, the International Standards Organization, and the TM Forum are pushing for interoperability and portability standards. "I think there is a safe prediction that we will have much more interoperability in the future right around the three- to five-year point. Probably closer to five, we will have that cloud of cloud people are talking about," Messina said [144].

Randy Garrett, program manager with the Defense Advanced Research Projects Agency's Information Innovation Office, who was also on the panel, said, "We will see a growth in the Internet of Things," referring to devices ranging from smartphones to automated sensors and non-computing devices connected to the internet.

An interconnected world has potential benefits, but it also creates new risks. For example, 10 years ago, there was no danger that somebody could remotely take over your car with a cyberattack. But a car today with onboard computers, a GPS receiver, and wireless connections is vulnerable. Someone can take over a car. They cannot steer it (unless we are talking about Google's driverless car), Garrett noted, but can do other things. "So when you take that possibility and spread it out, it makes you wonder what type of future world we will have if somebody can come in remotely change your heating or air conditioning or shut down your car."

"Still, a lot of future benefits will arise as a result of connected devices and access to more information such as the better tracking of the rise and spread of epidemics, a larger sampling of medicines or the ability to detect manufacturing defects," Garrett said [145].

References

[141] http://www.cloudcomputing-news.net/news/2013/dec/10/ibm-launches-cloud-clouds-offering-aims-stop-vendor-lockin/
[142] http://www.techopedia.com/definition/7756/intercloud

[143] http://www.cloudwards.net/news/ibm-offers-intercloud-storage-2914/

[144] http://www.techradar.com/us/news/internet/ibm-working-on-cloud-of-clouds-solution-to-limit-vendor-lock-in-1207375#null

[145] http://gcn.com/Articles/2013/05/31/Cloud-of-clouds-5-years-in-future.aspx?Page=3#

23

Myths and Facts About Cloud Computing

Cloud is recognized as facilitating "speed-to-market" – and for its ability to drive business agility. This is because cloud supports rapid experimentation and innovation by allowing companies to quickly try and even adopt new solutions without significant up-front costs. The cloud can be a highly agile wrapped around different systems, different behavior, and bringing it all together in an engagement cycle. By changing the way people interact with technology, cloud enables new forms of consumer engagement, expand collaboration across the value chain, and bring innovation to companies' core business models.

23.1 Types of Cloud Computing

- *Public cloud*: In public cloud, the computing infrastructure is hosted by the cloud vendor at the vendor's premises. The customer has no visibility and control over where the computing infrastructure is hosted. The computing infrastructure is shared between any organizations.

*   *Private cloud*: The computing infrastructure is dedicated to a particular organization and not shared with other organizations. Private clouds are more expensive and more secure when compared to public clouds. Private cloud is what used to be called your company network.

*   *Hybrid cloud*: Organizations may host critical applications on private clouds and applications with relatively fewer security concerns on the public cloud. The usage of both private and public clouds together is called hybrid cloud.

With all this in mind and the reality of cloud computing impacting businesses in all aspects and at all levels, there are myths surrounding cloud computing and clouding the reality of the cloud.

Myth #1: It is only for tech companies: Nothing is far from the truth as this myth; any company in the horizontal and vertical markets can use it including no matter what the size is.

Myth #2: Security is the biggest risk: Security measures used by well-known cloud vendors are often better than their clients; the cloud vendors have the resources and the skills to keep it up to date.

Myth #3: Everything works better in the cloud: Except old applications that were designed to run on dedicated servers, often difficult to run on the cloud.

Myth #4: It is always cheaper to run on the Cloud: It is not always cheaper to run on the cloud, but it can often be more cost efficient. Cloud works best for variable demands and workloads, where you have high demand at times but lower demand at others.

Myth #5: Cloud is harmful to the environment: There is no question that data centers consume huge amounts of energy. But when businesses move from on-site facilities to consolidated cloud data centers, it saves energy and cuts pollution.

Myth #6: Cloud costs jobs: Instead of taking jobs, it is, in fact, creating them; industry predictions suggest that by the end of 2015, cloud computing will have created more than 13 million jobs worldwide. It required a host of cloud-savvy experts whose skills and knowledge will maintain and strengthen growth and development.

Myth #7: Migrating into the cloud is more hassle than it is worth: If you work in partnership with a trusted and experienced hosting provider, it is a seamless process. It can all happen very quickly with minimal downtime.

Myth #8: Cloud is not for mission-critical use: Cloud computing can be used for all aspects of business including mission-critical applications for many reasons including less downtime, and auto backup.

Myth #9: Cloud is virtualization: Virtualization is software that manipulates hardware, while cloud computing refers to a service that results from that manipulation.

Myth #10: I will be caught by vendor "lock in": This is true only to the same extent of on-premise, traditional software. There would be nothing to stop businesses building their own applications and deal with more than one vendor [141].

23.2 The Promise of Cloud Computing

Understanding what is next for cloud computing is crucial for businesses at all levels because the cloud is not just for techies anymore. Managers are responding to the real opportunities that the cloud offers to develop new business models, forge closer ties with customers, and use the expertise of employees and partners. From a technology that was initially adopted for efficiency and cost savings, the cloud has emerged as a powerhouse of innovation throughout organizations.

The next generation of cloud computing will deliver value to the business faster by automating everything from request to deployment and configuration – and do so up and down the stack and across the entire infrastructure. Cloud computing is part of the "third platform" according to IDC along with mobility, big data analytics, and social business, which explains why many businesses adopted the cloud to create innovative industry solutions. Now cloud computing is moving the bar higher with the Internet of Things (IoT) which is built on the cloud for the cloud.

The next generation of cloud computing will deliver value to the business faster by automating everything from request to deployment and configuration – and do so up and down the stack and across the entire infrastructure. In order for the next generation of computing to achieve these goals, there are five platform requirements:

1. A management platform that engenders a high degree of service flexibility

2. A platform that can support multiple constituencies

3.   A platform that is not tied to a single infrastructure

4.   An intelligent platform

5.   A platform that is integrated with your existing enterprise management technology and processes

23.3 What is Next for Cloud Computing?

- *Introduction of cloud-of-clouds or intercloud*: A new model for cloud computing services based on the idea of combining many different individual clouds into one seamless mass in terms of on-demand operations. The intercloud would simply make sure that a cloud could use resources beyond its reach, by taking advantage of pre-existing contracts with other cloud providers [142].

- *Platforms-as-a-service continues to grow*: More companies will be looking to adopt PaaS solutions in the upcoming years. PaaS allows businesses to lower IT costs while speeding up application development through more efficient testing and deployment.

- *Graphics as a service*: Running high-end graphics applications typically requires massive hardware infrastructure, but cloud computing is changing that. With the emerging cloud-based graphics technologies, end-users will run graphically intense applications using nothing more than a web browser.

- *More hybrid cloud adoption*: Hybrid cloud is a combination of the private cloud and public cloud enabling IT to utilize on premise and cloud-based infrastructure seamlessly for cost reduction, bursting, disaster recovery, and other use cases. The key to hybrid cloud acceptance in the marketplace is providing this "seamless" capability for all applications, including those production applications that are core to the business.

- *Cloud as the innovation platform for mobile, social, and big data*: Cloud technology provides a common platform for mobile, social, and big data applications to cross pollinate as well as enhance and extend existing investments. Cloud as innovation platform will give businesses the agility to respond quickly to new innovations, e.g., wearable technology or speech and gesture interaction with applications.

- *The Internet of Things takes off*: Look for the industrial internet (a.k.a. the Internet of Things) to start transforming operations in few coming years, as solutions combining intelligent machines, big data analytics, and end-user applications begin to roll out across major industries. Cloud computing platforms will play a big role in creating the next generation of intelligent, software-defined machines that are operable and controllable entirely from centralized, remote locations.

- *Better identity management in the cloud*: Cloud services offer accessibility, convenience, high-power, and redundancy, but with cloud-based applications taking over businesses, there is a need to rethink security policies. Look for identity management solutions to bring new paradigms of security to the cloud.

- *More software-defined hardware*: In order for servers, storage, and networking equipment to behave like one big "machine," where applications can assume massive scalability, the entire infrastructure must be virtualized and centrally controllable, that is, software-defined. Ultimately, this trend goes beyond SDN (software-defined networks) to include every system in the data center. Advanced software control schemes pioneered by public cloud providers will continue to trickle down to the enterprise [143].

PART 5

Security

24

Zero-Day Vulnerability and Heuristic Analysis

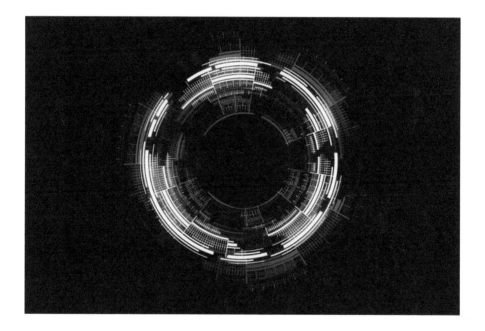

24.1 What is a Zero-Day Vulnerability?

A zero-day vulnerability refers to a hole in software that is unknown to the vendor. This security hole is then exploited by hackers before the vendor becomes aware and fixes it. Uses of zero-day attacks can include infiltrating malware, spyware, or allowing unwanted access to user information.

The term "zero day," also known as zero-day, refers to the unknown nature of the hole to those outside of the hackers, specifically, the developers. Once the vulnerability becomes known, a race begins for the developer, who must protect users [146].

24.2 Zero-Day Exploit

A zero-day exploit is one that takes advantage of security vulnerability on the *same day* that the vulnerability becomes generally known. There are zero days between the time the vulnerability is discovered and the first attack.

Ordinarily, when someone detects that a software program contains a potential security issue, that person or company will notify the software company (and sometimes the world at large) so that action can be taken. Given time, the software company can fix the code and distribute a patch or software update [147].

24.3 Zero-Day Threat

Zero-day attacks occur within a time frame, known as the *vulnerability window*. This extends from the first vulnerability exploit to the point at which a threat is countered. Attackers engineer malicious software (malware) to exploit common file types, compromise attacked systems, and steal valuable data. Zero-day attacks are carefully implemented for maximum damage – usually in the span of one day. The vulnerability window could range from a small period to multiple years.

24.4 Defending Against Zero-Day Threats

There is no method of detection for zero-day exploits that is 100% reliable; however, there are two things that could greatly help an administrator Figure 24.1.

The *first* is patch management. The effect of this method will be somewhat limited since the attack would still be unknown and no patch would be available to address the exploit. However, if all systems are up-to-date, the

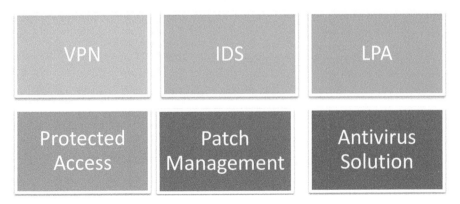

Figure 24.1 Defending against zero-day threats.

scope of attack might be limited and the attacker can only cause minimal damage while further threats are contained.

Furthermore, with a robust patch management and vulnerability scanning system in place, the administrator will receive notification as soon as the attack is made public and security companies implement vulnerability checks for it. These two important software solutions allow the administrator to take proactive action until a patch for that exploit is released. The administrator will also be notified when the patch for the zero-day attack is made public, thus minimizing the window of opportunity for an attack to take place.

The *second* option is to use a good antivirus solution. A zero-day attack does not become public knowledge for a period of time, and during that period, the antivirus program will not detect any file containing this specific vulnerability by using standard pattern analysis techniques.

However, effective antivirus solutions do not rely solely on antivirus definitions to detect threats. A good antivirus also uses a technique called *heuristics analysis*. This technique does not only look for certain patterns in a file, but it will also analyze what the file actually does during its normal execution. Depending on the file's behavior, the antivirus (AV) product may then classify the file as a virus if suspicious behavior is detected. This technique can help to detect a zero-day threat even though no one knows of the vulnerability's existence [148].

While antivirus solutions that use heuristic analyses can be a great weapon against zero-day malware, there is no guarantee that the malware behavior will always be classified as malicious. However, when AV is coupled with a strong patch management strategy, the administrator has a much stronger defense against infection by zero-day threats.

Other techniques used for early detection are as follows:

*   Use VPNs to protect the contents of individual transmissions

*   Deploy an intrusion detection system (IDS) (e.g., stateful firewall)

*   Introduce network access control to prevent rogue machines from gaining access to the network, in technical terms; least privilege access (LPA)

*   Lock down wireless access points and use a security scheme like Wi-Fi protected access for maximum protection against wireless-based attacks

24.5 What are Heuristics?

It is generally well-understood that antimalware (including antivirus) programs work by scanning files using signatures they already have. A signature could be as simple as a string (like using the "find" command in your word processor to locate a particular piece of text) or as complex as a tiny macro or subroutine which tells the scanning engine what to look for and where to find it.

Signature scanning works very well for detecting threats that have already been identified, but how do antimalware programs detect new, previously unseen threats? One of the methods used is *heuristics*.

Heuristic (from the Greek for "find" or "discover": the most popular/proper pronunciation is "hyoo-ris-tik") is an adjective for experience-based techniques that help in problem solving, learning, and discovery.

In computer science, a heuristic is an algorithm which consistently performs quickly and/or provides good results. But for antimalware software, heuristics can also have a more specialized meaning: heuristics refers to a set of rules – as opposed to a specific set of program instructions – used to detect malicious behavior without having to uniquely identify the program responsible for it, which is how a classic signature-based "virus scanner" works, i.e., identifying the specific computer virus or other programs.

The heuristic engine used by an antimalware program includes rules for the following:

- A program that tries to copy itself into other programs (in other words, a classic computer virus)

- A program that tries to write directly to the disk

- A program that tries to remain resident in memory after it has finished executing

- A program that decrypts itself when run (a method often used by malware to avoid signature scanners)

- A program that binds to a TCP/IP port and listens for instructions over a network connection (this is pretty much what a bot – also sometimes called drones or zombies – do)

- A program that attempts to manipulate (copy, delete, modify, rename, replace, and so forth) files that are required by the operating system

- A program that is similar to programs already known to be malicious

Some heuristic rules may have a heavier weight (and thus, score higher) than others, meaning that a match with one particular rule is more likely to indicate the presence of malicious software, as are multiple matches based on different rules.

Even more advanced heuristics might trace through the instructions in a program's code before passing it to the computer's processor for execution, allow the program to run in a virtual environment or "*sandbox*" to examine the behavior performed by and changes made to the virtual environment, and so forth. In effect, antimalware software can contain specialized emulators that allow it to "trick" a program into thinking it is actually running on the computer, instead of being examined by the antimalware software for potential threats.

A heuristic engine could be examining processes and structures in memory, the data portion (or payload) of packets traveling over a network, and so forth [149].

The advantage of heuristic analysis of code is that it can detect not just variants (modified forms) of existing malicious programs but new, previously unknown malicious programs, as well. Combined with other ways of looking for malware, such as *signature detection*, *behavioral monitoring*, and *reputation analysis*, heuristics can offer impressive accuracy. That is, correctly detecting a high proportion of real malware yet exhibiting a low false positive alarm rate as well, since misdiagnosing innocent files as malicious can cause severe problems.

References

[146] http://internet-security-suite-review.toptenreviews.com/premium-security-suites/what-is-heuristic-antivirus-detection-.html
[147] http://www.welivesecurity.com/2010/12/29/what-are-heuristics/
[148] http://www.gfi.com/blog/defending-zeroday-threats/
[149] http://www.techopedia.com/definition/27451/zero-day-threat

25

The Zero Trust Model

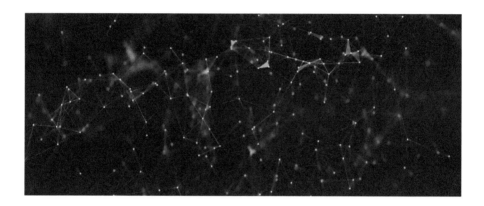

The zero trust model of information security simplifies how information security is conceptualized by assuming there are no longer "trusted" interfaces, applications, traffic, networks, or users. It takes the old model – "trust but verify" – and inverts it, because recent breaches have proven that when an organization trusts, it does not verify [155].

This model requires that the following rules be followed [155]:

- All resources must be accessed in a secure manner.
- Access control must be on a need-to-know basis and strictly enforced.
- Systems must verify and never trust.
- All traffic must be inspected, logged, and reviewed.
- Systems must be designed from the inside out instead of the outside in.

The zero-trust model has three key concepts:

- Ensure all resources are accessed securely regardless of location.
- Adopt a least privilege strategy and strictly enforce access control.
- Inspect and log all traffic.

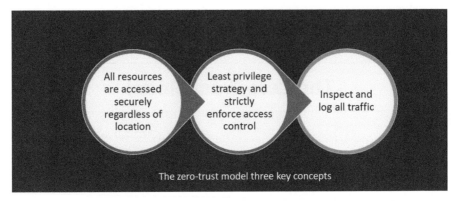

Figure 25.1   The zero-trust model three key concepts.

25.1 "Outside-In" to "Inside-Out" Attacks

According to a *Forrester Research* report, information security profession-als should readjust some widely held views on how to combat cyber risks. Security professionals emphasize strengthening the network perimeter, the report states, but evolving threats – such as increasing misuse of employee passwords and targeted attacks – mean executives need to start buffering internal networks. In the zero-trust security model, companies should also analyze employee access and internal network traffic. *One major recommen-dation* of the Forrester report is for companies to grant minimal employee access privileges. It also emphasizes the importance of log analysis; *another recommendation* is for increased use of tools that inspect the actual content, or data "packets," of internal traffic [150, 152].

Teams within enterprises, with and without the support of information technology management, are embracing new technologies in the constant quest to improve business and personal effectiveness and efficiency. These technologies include virtualization; cloud computing; converged data, voice, and video networks; Web 2.0 applications; social networking; smartphones; and tablets. In addition, the percentage of remote and mobile workers in orga-nizations continues to increase and reduce the value of physical perimeter controls [151].

The primary vector of attackers has shifted from *"outside-in"* to *"inside-out."* Formerly, the primary attack vector was to directly penetrate the enterprise at the network level through open ports and to exploit operat-ing system vulnerabilities. We call this attack methodology "outside-in." In "inside-out" attacks, the user inside the "protected" network reaching out to an external website can be just as vulnerable as the user accessing the internet from home [153, 154].

25.2 Zero Trust Recommendations

- Update network security with next-generation firewalls.

- Use a "sandbox" control to detect unknown threats in files.

- Establish protected enclaves to control user access to applications and resources.

- Use a specialized anti-phishing email protection service.

- Use threat intelligence to prioritize vulnerability remediation.

- Analyze logs using advanced machine learning algorithms to detect compromised and malicious users.

- Implement an incident management system to minimize the impact of individual incidents.

- Deploy a cloud services manager to discover, analyze, and control *shadow IT* (shadow IT is hardware or software within an enterprise that is not supported by the organization's central IT department).

- Monitor your partners' security postures using a cloud-based service.

- Deploy an enterprise key and certificate management system.

- Deploy a backup, cloud-based DDoS mitigation service.

- Deploy a non-signature-based endpoint malware detection control.

Just remember: the zero-trust model of information security means "verify and never trust."

References

[150] http://www.securitymanagement.com/article/zero-trust-model-007894
[151] http://www.securityweek.com/steps-implementing-zero-trust-network
[152] http://spyders.ca/reduce-risk-by-adopting-a-zero-trust-modelapproach-to-security/
[153] http://www.cymbel.com/zero-trust-recommendations/
[154] http://csrc.nist.gov/cyberframework/rfi_comments/040813_forrester_research.pdf
[155] https://go.forrester.com/research/

26

Cloud Computing Security

There is a broad set of policies, technologies, and controls deployed to protect data, applications, and the associated infrastructure of cloud computing.

Because of the cloud's very nature as a shared resource, identity management, privacy, and access control are of particular concern. With more organizations using cloud computing and associated cloud providers for data operations, proper security in these and other potentially vulnerable areas have become a priority for organizations contracting with a cloud computing provider.

Cloud computing security processes should address the security controls the cloud provider will incorporate to maintain the customer's data security, privacy, and compliance with necessary regulations. The processes will also likely include a business continuity and data backup plan in the case of a cloud security breach.

In the second half of 2013, *Forrester Research* conducted its usual Forrsights Hardware Survey and found enterprise hardware buyers more than willing to make use of cloud servers, but they were limiting their use because of unresolved concerns over security. In that survey, 73% of IT decision makers were concerned about public cloud security, and 51% were concerned about their own private cloud security.

26.1 Cloud Security Threats

According to *The Cloud Security Alliance*'s report, the biggest threats are as follows.

- *Data breaches*: Cloud computing introduces significant new avenues of attack. The absolute security of hypervisor (a virtual machine manager) operation and virtual machine operations is still to be proven. Clouds represent concentrations of corporate applications and data, and if any intruder penetrated far enough, who knows how many sensitive pieces of information will be exposed. "If a multitenant cloud service database is not properly designed, a flaw in one client's application could allow an attacker access not only to that client's data, but every other client's data as well," the report concluded.

- *Data loss*: A data breach is the result of a malicious and probably intrusive action. Small amounts of data were lost for some Amazon Web Service customers as its EC2 cloud suffered *"a remirroring storm"* due to human operator error on Easter weekend in 2011. And a data loss could occur intentionally in the event of a malicious attack.

- *Account or service traffic hijacking*: Account hijacking sounds too elementary to be a concern in the cloud. Phishing, exploitation of software vulnerabilities such as buffer overflow attacks, and loss of passwords and credentials can all lead to the loss of control over a user account, compromising the confidentiality, integrity, and availability of the services.

- *Insecure APIs*: The cloud era has brought about the contradiction of trying to make services available to millions while limiting any damage all these largely anonymous users might do to the service. The answer has been application programming interface, or API, that defines how a third party connects an application to the service and providing verification that the third party producing the application is who he says he is. Leading web developers, including ones from Twitter and Google, collaborated on specifying an open authorization service for web services that controls third party access. But security experts warn that there is no perfectly secure public API.

- *Denial of service*: Denial of service attacks are an old disrupter of online operations, but they remain a threat nevertheless. For cloud customers, experiencing a denial of service attack is like being caught in rush-hour traffic gridlock: there is no way to get to your destination, and there is nothing you can do about it except to sit and wait. When a denial of service attacks a customer's service in the cloud, it may impair service without shutting it down.

- *Malicious insiders*: Malicious insiders might seem to be a common threat. If one exists inside a large cloud organization, the hazards are magnified. One tactic cloud customers should use to protect themselves is to keep their encryption keys on their own premises, not in the cloud.

- *Abuse of cloud services*: Cloud computing brings large-scale, elastic services to enterprise users and hackers alike. It might take an attacker a year to crack an encryption key using his own limited hardware. But using an array of cloud servers, he might be able to crack it in minutes.

- *Insufficient due diligence*: Too many enterprises jump into the cloud without understanding the full scope of the undertaking. Without an understanding of the service providers' environment and protections, customers do not know what to expect in the way of incident response, encryption use, and security monitoring. Not knowing these factors means organizations are taking on unknown levels of risk in ways they may not even comprehend but that are a far departure from their current risks.

- *Shared technology*: In a multi-tenant environment, the compromise of a single component, such as the hypervisor, exposes more than just the compromised customer; rather, it exposes the entire environment to a potential of compromise and breach. The same could be said about other shared services, including CPU caches, a shared database service, or shared storage.

26.2 The Future

The cloud now represents not only concentrations of compute power and storage but also a concentration of security, given the potential for mischief or disaster if those centralized resources fall into the wrong hands. Whether it is a private cloud in the virtualized enterprise datacenter or a public cloud, new levels of "layered" security will need to be built in. Such security will need to operate in a highly automated fashion and be driven by well-crafted and relentlessly applied policies.

27

First Line of Defense for Cybersecurity: AI

The past few years were not great for cybersecurity; we saw a large number of high-profile cyberattacks, including Uber, Deloitte, Equifax, and the now infamous WannaCry ransomware attack. The frightening truth about increasing cyberattacks is that most businesses and the cybersecurity industry itself are not prepared. Despite the constant flow of security updates and patches, the number of attacks continues to rise [156].

Beyond the lack of preparedness on the business level, the cybersecurity workforce itself is also having an incredibly hard time keeping up with demand. By 2021, there are estimated to be an astounding 3.5 million unfilled cybersecurity positions worldwide; the current staff is overworked with an average of 52 hours a week, not an ideal situation to keep up with non-stop threats.

Given the state of cybersecurity today, the implementation of AI systems into the mix can serve as a real turning point. New AI algorithms use machine learning (ML) to adapt over time and make it easier to respond to cybersecurity risks. However, new generations of malware and cyberattacks can be difficult to detect with conventional cybersecurity protocols. They evolve over time; so more dynamic approaches are necessary.

Another great benefit of AI systems in cybersecurity is that they will free up an enormous amount of time for tech employees. Another way AI systems can help is by categorizing attacks based on threat level. While there is still a fair amount of work to be done here, but when machine learning principles are incorporated into your systems, they can actually adapt over time, giving you a dynamic edge over cyber criminals [157].

Unfortunately, there will always be limits of AI, and human–machine teams will be the key to solving increasingly complex cybersecurity challenges. But as our models become effective at detecting threats, bad actors will look for ways to confuse the models. It is a field called adversarial machine learning, or adversarial AI. Bad actors will study how the underlying models work and work to either confuse the models – what experts call poisoning the models, or machine learning poisoning (MLP) – or focus on a wide range of evasion techniques, essentially looking for ways they can circumvent the models.

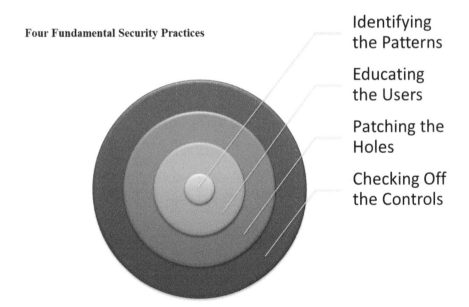

Four Fundamental Security Practices

Identifying the Patterns

Educating the Users

Patching the Holes

Checking Off the Controls

Figure 27.1   Four fundamental security practices.

27.1 Four Fundamental Security Practices

With all the hype surrounding AI, we tend to overlook a very important fact. The best defense against a potential AI cyberattack is rooted in maintaining a fundamental security posture that incorporates continuous monitoring, user education, diligent patch management, and basic configuration controls to address vulnerabilities. All are explained in the following.

27.1.1 Identifying the patterns

AI is all about patterns. Hackers, for example, look for patterns in server and firewall configurations, use of outdated operating systems, user actions, response tactics, and more. These patterns give them information about network vulnerabilities they can exploit.

Network administrators also look for patterns. In addition to scanning for patterns in the way hackers attempt intrusions, they are trying to identify potential anomalies like spikes in network traffic, irregular types of network traffic, unauthorized user logins, and other red flags.

By collecting data and monitoring the state of their network under normal operating conditions, administrators can set up their systems to automatically detect when something unusual takes place – a suspicious network login, for example, or access through a known bad IP. This fundamental security approach has worked extraordinarily well in preventing more traditional types of attacks, such as malware or phishing. It can also be used very effectively in deterring AI-enabled threats [158].

27.1.2 Educating the users

An organization could have the best monitoring systems in the world, but the work they do can all be undermined by a single employee clicking on the wrong email. Social engineering continues to be a large security challenge for businesses because workers easily can be tricked into clicking on suspicious attachments, emails, and links. Employees are considered by many as the *weakest links* in the security chain, as evidenced by a recent survey that found that careless and untrained insiders represented the top source of security threats.

Educating users on what not to do is just as important as putting security safeguards in place. Experts agree that routine user testing reinforces training. Agencies must also develop plans that require all employees to understand their individual roles in the battle for better security. And do not forget a response and recovery plan so that everyone knows what to do and

Figure 27.2 Challenges faced using AI in cybersecurity.

expect when a breach occurs. Test these plans for effectiveness. Do not wait for an exploit to find a hole in the process.

27.1.3 Patching the holes

Hackers know when a patch is released, and in addition to trying to find a way around that patch, they will not hesitate to test if an agency has implemented the fix. Not applying patches opens the door to potential attacks – and if the hacker is using AI, those attacks can come much faster and be even more insidious.

27.1.4 Checking off the controls

The Center for Internet Security (CIS) has issued a set of controls designed to provide agencies with a checklist for better security implementations. While there are 20 actions in total, implementing at least the top five – device inventories, software tracking, security configurations, vulnerability assessments, and control of administrative privileges – can eliminate roughly 85% of an organization's vulnerabilities. All of these practices – monitoring, user education, patch management, and adherence to CIS controls – can help agencies fortify themselves against even the most sophisticated AI attacks.

27.2 Challenges Faced by AI in Cybersecurity

27.2.1 AI-powered attacks

AI/machine learning (ML) software has the ability to "learn" from the consequences of past events in order to help predict and identify cybersecurity threats. According to a report by Webroot, AI is used by approximately 87% of US cybersecurity professionals. However, AI may prove to be a double-edged sword as 91% of security professionals are concerned that hackers will use AI to launch even more sophisticated cyberattacks.

For example, AI can be used to automate the collection of certain information – perhaps relating to a specific organization – which may be sourced from support forums, code repositories, social media platforms, and more. Additionally, AI may be able to assist hackers when it comes to cracking passwords by narrowing down the number of probable passwords based on geography, demographics, and other such factors [159].

27.2.2 More sandbox-evading malware

In recent years, sandboxing technology has become an increasingly popular method for detecting and preventing malware infections. However, cyber-criminals are finding more ways to evade this technology. For example, new strains of malware are able to recognize when they are inside a sandbox and wait until they are outside the sandbox before executing the malicious code.

27.2.3 Ransomware and IoT

We should be very careful not to underestimate the potential damage IoT ransomware could cause. For example, hackers may choose to target critical systems such as power grids. Should the victim fail to the pay the ransom within a short period of time, the attackers may choose to shut down the grid. Alternatively, they may choose to target factory lines, smart cars, and home appliances such as smart fridges, smart ovens, and more.

This fear was realized with a massive distributed denial of service attack that crippled the servers of services like Twitter, Netflix, NYTimes, and PayPal across the US on October 21, 2016. It is the result of an immense assault that involved millions of internet addresses and malicious software, according to Dyn, the prime victim of that attack. "One source of the traffic for the attacks was devices infected by the Mirai botnet." The attack comes amid heightened cybersecurity fears and a rising number of internet security breaches. Preliminary indications suggest that countless Internet of Things (IoT) devices that power everyday technology like closed-circuit cameras and smart-home devices were hijacked by the malware and used against the servers.

27.2.4 A rise of state-sponsored attacks

The rise of nation state cyberattacks is perhaps one of the most concerning areas of cybersecurity. Such attacks are usually politically motivated and go beyond financial gain. Instead, they are typically designed to acquire intelligence that can be used to obstruct the objectives of a given political entity. They may also be used to target electronic voting systems in order to manipulate public opinion in some way.

As you would expect, state-sponsored attacks are targeted, sophisticated, and well-funded and have the potential to be incredibly disruptive. Of course, given the level of expertise and finance that is behind these attacks, they may prove very difficult to protect against. Governments must ensure that their internal networks are isolated from the internet and that extensive security checks are carried out on all staff members. Likewise, staff will need to be sufficiently trained to spot potential attacks.

27.2.5 Shortage of skilled staff

By practically every measure, cybersecurity threats are growing more numerous and sophisticated each passing day, a state of affairs that does not bode well for an IT industry struggling with a security skills shortage. With less security talent to go around, there is a growing concern that businesses will lack the expertise to thwart network attacks and prevent data breaches in the years ahead.

27.2.6 IT infrastructure

A modern enterprise has just too many IT systems, spread across geographies. Manual tracking of the health of these systems, even when they operate in a highly integrated manner, poses massive challenges. For most businesses, the only practical method of embracing advanced (and expensive) cybersecurity technologies is to prioritize their IT systems and cover those that they deem critical for business continuity. Currently, cybersecurity is reactive. That is to say that in most cases, it helps alert IT staff about data breaches, identity theft, suspicious applications, and suspicious activities. So, cybersecurity is currently more of an enabler of disaster management and mitigation. This leaves a crucial question unanswered – what about not letting cybercrime happen at all?

27.3 The Future of Cybersecurity and AI

In the security world, AI has a very clear-cut potential for good. The industry is notoriously unbalanced, with the bad actors getting to pick from thousands of vulnerabilities to launch their attacks, along with deploying an ever-increasing arsenal of tools to evade detection once they have breached a system. While they only have to be successful once, the security experts tasked with defending a system have to stop every attack, every time.

With the advanced resources, intelligence and motivation to complete an attack found in high level attacks, and the sheer number of attacks happening every day, victory eventually becomes impossible for the defenders.

The analytical speed and power of our dream security AI would be able to tip these scales at last, leveling the playing field for the security practitioners who currently have to constantly defend at scale against attackers who can pick a weak spot at their leisure. Instead, even the well-planned and concealed attacks could be quickly found and defeated.

Of course, such a perfect security AI is some way off. Not only would this AI need to be a bona fide simulated mind that can pass the Turing test, it would also need to be a fully trained cybersecurity professional, capable of replicating the decisions made by the most experienced security engineer but on a vast scale.

Before we reach the brilliant AI seen in Sci-Fi, we need to go through some fairly testing stages – although these still have huge value in themselves. Some truly astounding breakthroughs are happening all the time. When it matures as a technology, it will be one of the most astounding developments in history, changing the human condition in ways similar to and bigger than electricity, flight, and the internet, because we are entering the AI era [160].

References

[156] https://www.csoonline.com/article/3250086/data-protection/7-cyber-security-trends-to-watch-out-for-in-2018.html
[157] https://gcn.com/articles/2018/01/05/ai-cybersecurity.aspx
[158] https://www.darkreading.com/threat-intelligence/ai-in-cybersecurity-where-we-stand-and-where-we-need-to-go/a/d-id/1330787?
[159] https://www.itproportal.com/features/cyber-security-ai-is-almost-here-but-where-does-that-leave-us-humans/
[160] https://www.linkedin.com/pulse/wake-up-call-iot-ahmed-banafa

28

Second Line of Defense for Cybersecurity: Blockchain

AI as the first line of defense for cybersecurity, the goal was to keep the cyber-criminals at bay, but in case they managed to get in and infiltrate the network, we need to initiate the second line of defense – blockchain. With the fact that cybercrime and cybersecurity attacks hardly seem to be out of the news these days and the threat is growing globally. Nobody would appear immune to malicious and offensive acts targeting computer networks, infrastructures, and personal computer devices. Firms clearly must invest to stay resilient. Gauging the exact size of cybercrime and putting a precise

US dollar value on it is nonetheless tricky. But one thing we can be sure about is that the number is big and probably larger than the statistics reveal [161].

The global figure for cyber breaches had been put at around $200 billion annually.

New blockchain platforms are stepping up to address security concerns in the face of recent breaches. Since these platforms are not controlled by a singular entity, they can help ease the concerns created by a spree of recent breach disclosures. Services built on top of blockchain have the potential to inspire renewed trust due to the transparency built into the technology.

Developments in blockchain have expanded beyond record-keeping and cryptocurrencies. The integration of *smart contract* development in blockchain platforms has ushered in a wider set of applications, including cybersecurity.

By using blockchain, transaction details are kept both transparent and secure. Blockchain's decentralized and distributed network also helps businesses to avoid a single point of failure, making it difficult for malicious parties to steal or tamper with business data.

Transactions in the blockchain can be audited and traced. In addition, public blockchains rely on distributed network to run, thus eliminating a single point of control. For attackers, it is much more difficult to attack a large number of peers distributed globally as opposed to a centralized data center [162].

28.1 Implementing Blockchain in Cybersecurity

Since a blockchain system is protected with the help of ledgers and cryptographic keys, attacking and manipulating it becomes extremely difficult. Blockchain decentralizes the systems by distributing ledger data on several systems rather than storing them on one single network. This allows the technology to focus on gathering data rather than worrying about any data being stolen. Thus, decentralization has led to an improved efficiency in blockchain-operated systems.

For a blockchain system to be penetrated, the attacker must intrude into every system on the network to manipulate the data that is stored on the network. The number of systems stored on every network can be in millions. Since domain editing rights are only given to those who require them, the hacker will not get the right to edit and manipulate the data even after hacking a million systems. Since such manipulation of data on the network has never taken place on the blockchain, it is not an easy task for any attacker.

While we store our data on a blockchain system, the threat of a possible hack gets eliminated. Every time our data is stored or inserted into blockchain

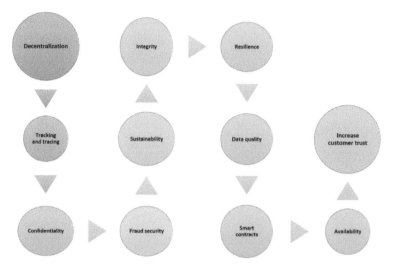

Figure 28.1 Advantages of using blockchain in cybersecurity.

ledgers, a new block is created. This block further stores a key that is cryptographically created. This key becomes the unlocking key for the next record that is to be stored onto the ledger. In this manner, the data is extremely secure.

Furthermore, the hashing feature of blockchain technology is one of its underlying qualities that make it such a prominent technology. Using cryptography and the hashing algorithm, blockchain technology converts the data stored in our ledgers. This hash encrypts the data and stores it in such a language that the data can only be decrypted using keys stored in the systems. Other than cybersecurity, blockchain has many applications in several fields that help in maintaining and securing data. The fields where this technology is already showing its ability are finance, supply chain management, and blockchain-enabled smart contracts.

28.2 Advantages of using Blockchain in Cybersecurity [163]

The main advantages of blockchain technology for cybersecurity are the following.

28.2.1 Decentralization

Thanks to the peer-to-peer network, there is no need for third-party verification, as any user can see network transactions.

28.2.2 Tracking and tracing

All transactions in blockchains are digitally signed and time-stamped; so network users can easily trace the history of transactions and track accounts at any historical moment. This feature also allows a company to have valid information about assets or product distribution.

28.2.3 Confidentiality

The confidentiality of network members is high due to the public-key cryptography that authenticates users and encrypts their transactions.

28.2.4 Fraud security

In the event of a hack, it is easy to define malicious behavior due to the peer-to-peer connections and distributed consensus. As of today, blockchains are considered technically "unhackable," as attackers can impact a network only by getting control of 51% of the network nodes.

28.2.5 Sustainability

Blockchain technology has no single point of failure, which means that even in the case of DDoS attacks, the system will operate as normal, thanks to multiple copies of the ledger.

28.2.6 Integrity

The distributed ledger ensures the protection of data against modification or destruction. Besides, the technology ensures the authenticity and irreversibility of completed transactions. Encrypted blocks contain immutable data that is resistant to hacking.

28.2.7 Resilience

The peer-to-peer nature of the technology ensures that the network will operate round-the-clock even if some nodes are offline or under attack. In the event of an attack, a company can make certain nodes redundant and operate as usual.

28.2.8 Data quality

Blockchain technology cannot improve the quality of your data, but it can guarantee the accuracy and quality of data after it is encrypted in the blockchain.

Figure 28.2   Disadvantages of using blockchain in cybersecurity.

28.2.9 Smart contracts

Software programs that are based on the ledger. These programs ensure the execution of contract terms and verify parties. Blockchain technology can significantly increase the security standards for smart contracts, as it minimizes the risks of cyberattacks and bugs.

28.2.10 Availability

There is no need to store your sensitive data in one place, as blockchain technology allows you to have multiple copies of your data that are always available to network users.

28.2.11 Increased customer trust

Your clients will trust you more if you can ensure a high level of data security. Moreover, blockchain technology allows you to provide your clients with information about your products and services instantly.

28.3 Disadvantages of using Blockchain in Cybersecurity

28.3.1 Irreversibility

There is a risk that encrypted data may be irrecoverable in case a user loses or forgets the private key necessary to decrypt it.

28.3.2 Storage limits

Each block can contain no more than 1 Mb of data, and a blockchain can handle only seven transactions per second in average.

28.3.3 Risk of cyberattacks

Though the technology greatly reduces the risk of malicious intervention, it is still not a panacea to all cyber threats. If attackers manage to exploit the majority of your network, you may lose your entire database.

28.3.4 Adaptability challenges

Though blockchain technology can be applied to almost any business, companies may face difficulties integrating it. Blockchain applications can also require complete replacement of existing systems; so companies should consider this before implementing the blockchain technology.

28.3.5 High operation costs

Running blockchain technology requires substantial computing power, which may lead to high marginal costs in comparison with existing systems.

28.3.6 Blockchain literacy

There are still not enough developers with experience in blockchain technology and with deep knowledge of cryptography.

28.4 Conclusion

Blockchain's decentralized approach to cybersecurity can be seen as a fresh take on the issues that the industry faces today. The market could only use more solutions to combat the threats of cyberattacks. And the use of blockchain may yet address the vulnerabilities and limitations of current security approaches and solutions.

Throwing constant pots of money at the problem and knee-jerk reactions is not the answer. Firms need to sort out their governance, awareness, and organizational culture and critically look at the business purpose and processes before they invest in systems to combat cybercrime.

The roster of these new services provided by blockchain may be limited for now, and, of course, they face incumbent players in the cybersecurity space. But this only offers further opportunity for other ventures to cover other key areas of cybersecurity. Blockchain also transcends borders and nationalities, which should inspire trust in users. And, with the growth of these new solutions, the industry may yet restore some of the public's trust they may have lost in the midst of all these issues.

Overall, blockchain technology is a breakthrough in cybersecurity, as it can ensure the highest level of data confidentiality, availability, and security. However, the complexity of the technology may cause difficulties with development and real-world use.

Implementation of blockchain applications requires comprehensive and enterprise- and risk-based approaches that capitalize on cybersecurity risk frameworks, best practices, and cybersecurity assurance services to mitigate risks. In addition, cyber intelligence capabilities, such as cognitive security, threat modeling, and artificial intelligence, can help proactively predict cyber threats to create counter measures; that is why AI is considered as the first line of defense while blockchain is the second line [164].

References

[161] https://www.ibm.com/blogs/insights-on-business/government/convergence-blockchain-cybersecurity/

[162] https://www.forbes.com/sites/rogeraitken/2017/11/13/new-blockchain-platforms-emerge-to-fight-cybercrime-secure-the-future/#25bdc5468adc

[163] http://www.technologyrecord.com/Article/cybersecurity-via-blockchain-the-pros-and-cons-62035

[164] https://www.allerin.com/blog/blockchain-cybersecurity

29

Network Security Needs Big Data

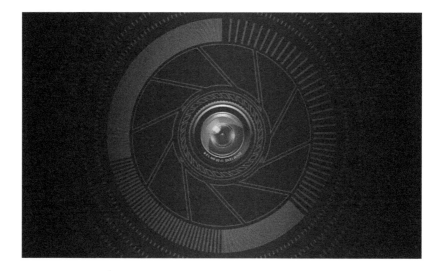

There are two types of organizations now: those that have been breached and those that just do not know it yet. As attacks have become too sophisticated for signature-based detection, there is a need for solutions that quickly notice anomalous and potentially dangerous behavior to prevent breaches or – failing that – detect malicious behavior once a breach has occurred, and minimize its impact, as *Neill Occhiogrosso* mentioned in his excellent article about this topic.

The second half of 2014 witnessed serious security incidents starting with Heartbleed, Bash Bug (Shellshock) to the recent Poodle bug; add to that the highly publicized security breaches at Target, Home Depot, K-Mart, and Chase. This raises the old question or quest: can we ever have a perfect secure network? The quick answer is "no"; but not too fast – there are ways to minimize risks and lower vulnerabilities of computer networks to the lowest possible level.

The traditional approach to network security is failing. According to the 2014 Cyberthreat Defense Report, more than 60% of organizations fell, victim to one or more successful cyberattacks. Given the extent to which today's organizations continue to rely on perimeter-centric strategies, this finding should come as no surprise. Studies have shown that between 66% and 90% of data breaches are identified not by organizations that are breached but by third-party organizations. The simple truth of the matter is that perimeter-based approaches to security are no longer effective.

According to the *Forrester Research* report, information security professionals should readjust some widely held views on how to combat cyber risks. Security professionals emphasize strengthening the network perimeter, the report states, but evolving threats – such as increasing misuse of employee passwords and targeted attacks – mean executives need to start buffering internal networks. Teams within enterprises, with and without the support of information technology management, are embracing new technologies in the constant quest to improve business and personal effectiveness and efficiency. These technologies include virtualization; cloud computing; converged data, voice, and video networks; Web 2.0 applications; social networking; smartphones; and tablets (BYOD). In addition, the percentage of remote and mobile workers in organizations continues to increase and reduce the value of physical perimeter controls proving that the "disconnect" between the security and network operations teams is at the heart of the problem. So what is the solution? One strong candidate in answering these questions is zero trust model (ZTM).

29.1 Zero Trust Model (ZTM)

"Zero trust" is an aggressive model of network security that monitors every piece of data possible, assuming that every file is a potential threat .The zero trust model of information security requires that all resources must be accessed in a secure manner, access control must be on a need-to-know basis and strictly enforced, systems must verify and never trust, all traffic must be inspected, logged, and reviewed, and systems must be designed from the inside out instead of the outside in. It simplifies how information security is conceptualized by assuming there are no longer "trusted" interfaces, applications, traffic, networks, or users. It takes the old model – "trust but verify" – and inverts it, because recent breaches have proven that when an organization trusts, it does not verify. This model was initially developed by *John Kindervag* of *Forrester Research* and popularized as a necessary evolution of traditional overlay security models.

In the "zero trust security model," companies should also analyze employee access and internal network traffic and grant minimal employee access privileges. It also emphasizes the importance of log analysis and increased use of tools that inspect the actual content or data "packets," of internal traffic "sandbox control."

A commissioned study conducted by Forrester Consulting on behalf of IBM results some interesting outcomes: many firms today are already on the path to support the zero trust model. Respondents of the survey indicate that many have already adopted key zero trust concepts today, whether they are aware of zero trust or not. This is encouraging. Implementation of the zero trust model then becomes less of a stretch for companies and more of an extension of the activities currently in place. Anywhere from 58% to 83% of respondents are already behaving in ways that support zero trust concepts, depending on activity (e.g., logging and inspecting all network traffic).

29.2 Big Data and ZTM

The convergence of big data and network security is a direct product of "applied big data" and it is a prime example of using analytics technologies to tackle a current business problem such as cyberattacks. Using ZTM will generate enormous volume of real-time data to analysis, which will have IT managers drowning in log files, vulnerability scan reports, alerts, reports, and more, but the data is not actionable at that stage. The magic in using big data analytics is in analyzing this data to give IT managers a comprehensive view of their security landscape, and exposing what is at risk, how severe the risk is, how important the asset is, and how to fix it. A natural progression of the use of analytics is to track and protect business assets regardless of the location as the perimeter of the network expanding with BYOD and the use of cloud technologies.

A promising approach in using big data is to apply *behavioral analytics* to data already resident in networks to prevent a broad range of suspicious activity. This is just one example of applying data science to existing data sets to address more nebulous threats, and generating profiles to anticipate future attacks.

Research firm Gartner said that big data analytics will play a crucial role in detecting cyberattacks. By 2020, more than 70% of global firms will adopt big data analytics for at least one security and fraud detection use case, up from current 8%. Going forward, big data will have an impact that will change most of the product categories in the field of computer network security including solutions, network monitoring, authentication and authorization of users, identity management, fraud detection, and systems of governance, risk, and compliance. Big data will change also the nature of the security controls as conventional firewalls, antimalware, and data loss prevention. In coming years, the tools of data analysis will evolve further to enable a number of advanced predictive capabilities and automated controls in real time.

Finally, the use of big data analytics in network security needs efficient data capture and analysis that can look broadly and historically across an infrastructure, sometimes trailing several months, to see when and how a breach occurred, and what the consequences were. This process involves great volume, variety, and velocity of data.

It is an open field for companies to introduce new products, services, and harvest the profit.

PART 6

Blockchain

30

Blockchain Technology and COVID-19

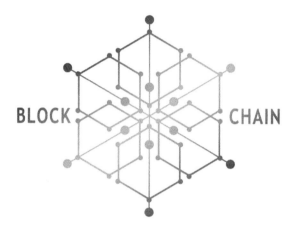

The COVID-19 coronavirus has impacted countries, communities, and individuals in countless ways, from school closures to healthcare insurance issues not to undermined loss of lives Figure 30.1. As governments scramble to address these problems, different solutions based on blockchain technologies have sprung up to help deal with the worldwide health crisis [166].

A blockchain is an essential tool for establishing an efficient and transparent healthcare business model based on higher degrees of accuracy and trust because technology is a tamper-proof public ledger. Blockchain will surely not prevent the emergence of new viruses itself, but what it can do is create the first line of rapid protection through a network of connected devices whose primary goal is to remain alert about disease outbreaks. Therefore, the use of blockchain-enabled platforms can help prevent these pandemics by enabling early detection of epidemics, fast-tracking drug trials, and impact management of outbreaks and treatment [173].

But before we explore in detail the possible ways of using blockchain to help in fighting this invisible enemy, we need to understand some of the challenges defining this deadly virus.

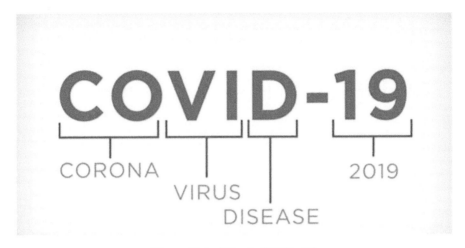

Figure 30.1   What is COVID-19?

30.1 Major Challenges of COVID-19

- One major issue is how prepared the world's health systems are to respond to this outbreak

- Tracking a huge population of infectious patients to stop epidemics

- Another is the immediate requirement for developing better diagnostics, vaccines, and targeted therapeutics

- Misinformation and conspiracy theories spread through social media platforms

- Various limitations while accessing the tools when required

- No adequate measures to adopt in a crisis situation [168, 171, 172]

30.2 Can Blockchain Help in Preventing Pandemics?

With blockchain, we can share any transaction/information, real time, between relevant parties present as nodes in the chain, in a secure and immutable fashion. In this case, had there been a blockchain where WHO, Health Ministry of each country and may be even relevant nodal hospitals of each country, were connected, sharing real-time information, about any new communicable disease, then the world might have woken up much earlier. We might have seen travel restrictions given sooner, quarantining policies set sooner, and social distancing implemented faster. And maybe fewer countries would have got impacted Figure. 30.2.

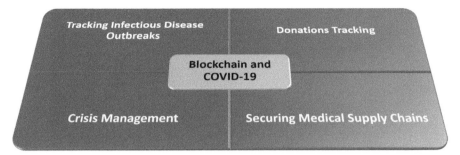

Figure 30.2 Blockchain applications in fighting COVID-19.

What every country is doing now fighting this pandemic would have been restricted to fewer countries and in a much smaller scale. The usage of a blockchain to share the information early on might have saved the world a lot of pain.

The world had not seen anything like COVID-19 pandemic before in the recent history. Today, we need to take a hard look at the reporting infrastructure available for communicable diseases, both technology and regulations, and improve upon that, such that we do not need to face another pandemic like this in the future [173].

30.3 Tracking Infectious Disease Outbreaks

Blockchain can be used for tracking public health data surveillance, particularly for infectious disease outbreaks such as COVID-19. With increased blockchain transparency, it will result in more accurate reporting and efficient responses. Blockchain can help develop treatments swiftly as they would allow for rapid processing of data, thus enabling early detection of symptoms before they spread to the level of epidemics.

Additionally, this will enable government agencies to keep track of the virus activity, of patients, suspected new cases, and more [173].

30.4 Donations Tracking

As trust is one of the major issues in donations, blockchain has a solution for this issue.

There has been a concern that the millions of dollars being donated for the public are not being put to use where needed.

With the help of blockchain capabilities, donors can see where funds are most urgently required and can track their donations until they are provided with a verification that their contributions have been received to the victims. Blockchain would enable transparency for the general public to understand how their donations have been used and its progress [9].

30.5 Crisis Management

Blockchain could also manage a crisis situation. It could instantly alert the public about the coronavirus by global institutes like the World Health Organization (WHO) using smart contracts concept.

Not only can it alert, but blockchain could also enable to provide governments with recommendations about how to contain the virus. It could offer a secure platform where all the concerning authorities such as governments, medical professionals, media, health organizations, media, and others can update each other about the situation and prevent it from worsening further [171].

30.6 Securing Medical Supply Chains

Blockchain has already proven its success stories as a supply chain management tool in various industries; similarly, blockchain could also be beneficial in tracking and tracing medical supply chains.

Blockchain-based platforms can be useful in reviewing, recording, and tracking of demand, supplies, and logistics of epidemic prevention materials. As supply chains involve multiple parties, the entire process of record and verification is tamper-proof by every party, while also allowing anyone to track the process.

This technology could help streamline medical supply chains, ensuring that doctors and patients have access to the tools whenever they need them, and restraining contaminated items from reaching stores [170, 173].

30.7 WHO and Blockchain Technology

The World Health Organization (WHO) is working with blockchain and other tech companies on a program to help convey data about the ongoing COVID-19 pandemic, named MiPasa.

The program is a distributed ledger technology (DLT) that will hopefully help with early detection of the virus and identifying carriers and hotspots.

MiPasa is built on top of Hyperledger Fabric in partnership with IBM, computer firm Oracle, enterprise blockchain platform HACERA, and IT corporation Microsoft. It purports to be "fully private" and share information between need-to-know organizations like state authorities and health officials.

Described by creators as "an information highway," MiPasa cross-references siloed location data with health information. It promises to protect patient privacy and to help monitor local and global trends such as the virus that has now sent the world spiraling into chaos and uncertainty in recent weeks.

The U.S., European, and Chinese Centers for Disease Control and Prevention, the Hong Kong Department of Health, the Government of Canada, and China's National Health Commission have all worked with the project [168, 169, 173].

References

[165] https://btcmanager.com/us-authorities-blockchain-covid-19-critical-services/?q=/us-authorities-blockchain-covid-19-critical-services/&

[166] https://www.govtech.com/products/Blockchain-Emerges-as-Useful-Tool-in-Fight-Against-Coronavirus.html

[167] https://www.expresscomputer.in/blockchain/could-blockchain-be-the-solution-for-surveillance-and-reporting-of-the-covid-19-pandemic/51670/

[168] https://www.ibm.com/blogs/blockchain/2020/03/mipasa-project-and-ibm-blockchain-team-on-open-data-platform-to-support-covid-19-response/

[169] https://mipasa.org/about/

[170] https://www.ledgerinsights.com/us-homeland-security-lists-blockchain-as-covid-19-critical-service/

[171] https://www.pymnts.com/blockchain/bitcoin/2020/bitcoin-daily-who-debuts-mipasa-blockchain-to-share-covid-19-data-coinbases-retail-payments-portal-passes-200m-transactions-processed/

[172] https://www.rollcall.com/2020/03/31/blockchain-could-transform-supply-chains-aid-in-covid-19-fight/

[173] https://www.blockchain-council.org/blockchain/how-blockchain-can-solve-major-challenges-of-covid-19-faced-by-healthcare-sectors/

31

How Blockchain is Revolutionizing Crowdfunding

According to experts, there are five key benefits of crowdfunding platforms: *efficiency, reach, easier presentation, built-in PR and marketing, and near-immediate validation of concept*, which explains why crowdfunding has become an extremely useful alternative to venture capital (VC), and has also allowed non-traditional projects, such as those started by in-need families or hopeful creatives, a new audience to pitch their cause. To date, $34 billion has been raised through crowdfunding initiatives, adding roughly $65 billion to the global economy in line with projections that show a possible $90 billion valuation for all crowdfunding sources, surpassing venture capital funding in the process [175].

31.1 Limitations of Current Crowdfunding Platforms Figure 31.1

1. *High fees*: Crowdfunding platforms take a fee for every project listed. Sometimes, this is a flat fee while others require a percentage of the total proceeds raised by contributors. This cuts into the availability of

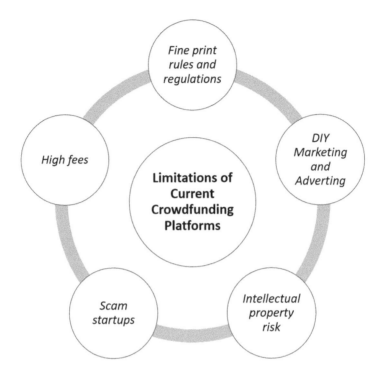

Figure 31.1   Limitations of current crowdfunding platforms.

funds and strains the fundraising process when startups are looking for every single dollar to help.

2. *Fine print rules and regulations*: Not all platforms accept services as a possible project and demand real tangible products; such a mindset cripples innovation and narrows the horizon of new products and services.

3. *DIY marketing and advertising*: With few exceptions, crowdfunding platforms will not help with spreading the word about new startups, which means startups need to pay for marketing and advertising yet another strain on limited funds available for them and take their focus from innovation and creativity.

4. *Scam startups*: In some cases, startups turn up as scams and produce nothing, leaving investors with empty hands and no way to get their money back.

5. *Intellectual property risk*: In some cases, startups have no protection of their IP, leaving them exposed to experience investors who can take the idea and enter the market early with all the resources they have.

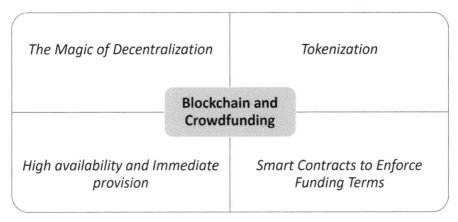

Figure 31.2 Blockchain and crowdfunding.

With all the above limitations of current crowdfunding platforms, blockchain technology, among all its benefits, can be best put to use by providing provable milestones as contingencies for giving, with *smart contracts* releasing funds only once milestones establish that the money is being used the way that it is said to be. By providing greater oversight into individual campaigns and reducing the amount of trust required to donate in good conscience, crowdfunding can become an even more legitimate means of funding a vast spectrum of projects and causes [175].

31.2 How Blockchain Helps Crowdfunding Figure 31.2

1. *The magic of decentralization*: Startups are not going to rely on any platform or combination of platforms to enable creators to raise funds. Startups no longer are beholden to the rules, regulations, and whims of the most popular crowdfunding platforms on the internet. Literally, any project has a chance of getting visibility and getting funded. It also eliminates the problem of fees. While blockchain upkeep does cost a bit of money, it will cut back drastically on transaction fees. This makes crowdfunding less expensive for creators and investors [174].

2. *Tokenization:* Instead of using crowdfunding to enable preorders of upcoming tangible products, blockchain could rely on asset tokenization to provide investors with equity or some similar concept of ownership, for example, initial coin offering (ICO). That way, investors will see success proportional to the eventual success of the company. This could potentially open whole new worlds of investment opportunity. Startups could save money on hiring employees by compensating them

partially in fractional ownership of the business, converting it into an employee-owned enterprise. Asset tokens become their own form of currency in this model, enabling organizations to do more like hire professionals like marketers and advertisers [174]

3. *High availability and immediate provision*: Any project using a blockchain-based crowdfunding model can potentially get funded. Also, any person with an internet connection can contribute to those projects. Blockchain-based crowdfunders would not have to worry about the "frauds" that have plagued modern-day crowdfunding projects. Instead contributors will immediately receive fractional enterprise or product ownership [174].

4. *Smart contracts to enforce funding terms*: There are several ways in which blockchain-enabled smart contracts could provide greater accountability in crowdfunding. Primarily, these contracts would provide built-in milestones that would prevent funds from being released without provenance as to a project or campaign's legitimacy. This would prevent large sums of money from being squandered by those who are either ill-intended or not qualified to be running a crowdfunding campaign in the first place [175].

References

[174] https://due.com/blog/a-new-era-of-crowdfunding-blockchain/
[175] https://www.disruptordaily.com/blockchain-use-cases-crowdfunding/

32

Blockchain Technology and Supply Chain Management

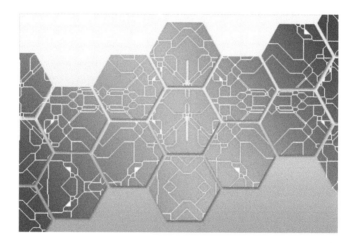

Managing today's supply chains is extremely complex. For many products, the supply chain can span over hundreds of stages; multiple geographical (international) locations and a multitude of invoices and payments have several individuals and entities involved, and extend over months of time. Due to the complexity and lack of transparency of the current supply chains, there is high interest in how blockchains might transform the supply chain and logistics industry [177].

This interest rose from the long list of issues with current supply chain management (SCM) including the following [176]:

* Difficulty of tracking

* Lack of trust

* High costs: procurement costs, transportation costs, inventory costs, and quality costs

* Globalization barriers

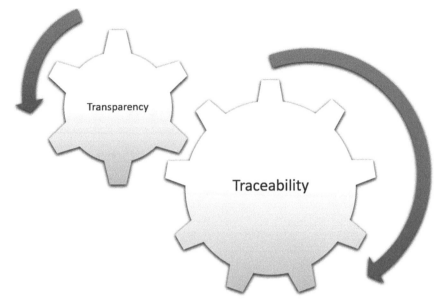

Figure 32.1   Blockchain technology and supply chain management.

32.1 Blockchain and SCM

Blockchain technology and supply chain management systems were built for each other in many ways. In fact, several of the flaws of the current supply chains can be easily relieved by using blockchain technology. Supply chain management (SCM) is one of the foremost industries that blockchain can disrupt and change for the better [176].

With blockchain technology properties of *decentralization, transparency*, and *immutability*, it is the perfect tool to save the supply chain management industry. Subsequently, blockchain can increases the efficiency and transparency of supply chains and positively impact everything from warehousing to delivery to payment. Most importantly, blockchain provides *consensus* – there is no dispute in the chain regarding transactions because all entities on the chain have the same version of the ledger [179].

Blockchain can have a big impact on SCM in two dimensions: *traceability* and *transparency*.

Traceability: Blockchain improves operational efficiency by mapping and visualizing enterprise supply chains. A growing number of consumers demand sourcing information about the products they buy. Blockchain helps organizations understand their supply chain and engage consumers with real, verifiable, and immutable data [3].

Transparency: Blockchain builds trust by capturing key data points, such as certifications and claims, and then provides open access to this data publicly. Once registered on the blockchain, its authenticity can be verified by a third party. The information can be updated and validated in real time. Additionally, the strong security from its innate cryptography will eliminate unnecessary audits, saving copious amounts of time and money [3].

Applying blockchain technology to SCM can result in tremendous benefits, including the following [178]:

• Less time delays

• Less human error

• Less costs

32.2 Applications of Blockchain in SCM

Walmart, for example, is using IBM's Food Trust Blockchain System to keep track of its meat products and its sources and the blockchain records where each piece of meat came from, processed, stored, and its sell-by-date. Unilever, Nestle, Tyson, and Dole also use blockchain for similar purposes [178].

BHP Billiton, the world's largest mining firm, uses blockchain to better track and record data throughout the mining process with its vendors. It not only increases efficiency internally but also allows the company to have more effective communication with its partners [178].

De Beers, the diamond-giant, uses blockchain technology to track stones from the point they are mined right up to the point they are sold to consumers. This ensures that the company avoids "conflict" or "blood diamonds" and assures the consumers that they are buying the genuine piece [178].

References

[176] https://blockgeeks.com/guides/Blockchain-and-supply-chain/
[177] https://www.forbes.com/sites/bernardmarr/2018/03/23/how-Blockchain-will-transform-the-supply-chain-and-logistics-industry/#c7c357e5fecd
[178] https://consensys.net/Blockchain-use-cases/supply-chain-management/
[179] https://www.technologyreview.com/2017/01/05/5880/a-secure-model-of-iot-with-blockchain/

PART 7

IoT

33

IoT and COVID-19

COVID-19 has impacted countries, communities, and individuals in count-less ways, from business and school closures to job losses, not to undermine loss of lives. As governments scramble to address these problems, different solutions based on technologies like IoT have sprung up to help in dealing with this worldwide health crisis. As a result, COVID-19 may well have been the ultimate catalyst of the Internet of Things (IoT) [182].

Internet of Things (IoT) platforms revenue will reach $66 billion in 2020, a 20% increase over last year's figure. The increase in revenue will be generated, for example, by businesses seeking greater resilience in areas including supply chain and asset management, against external factors such as the disruption caused by the global COVID-19 pandemic. That will enable the IoT market to overcome the anticipated widespread economic disruption over 2020 and beyond. Meanwhile, connected solutions are proving their worth in today's crisis, making them a critical part of many organizations' near-term technology roadmap [180].

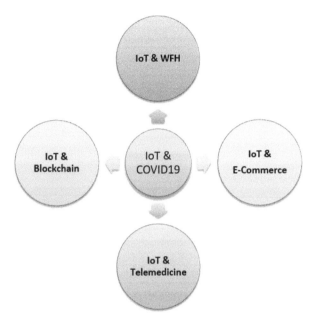

Figure 33.1 IoT and COVID-19.

In the following, we summarize some of the areas where IoT will flourish because of the COVID-19 impact.

33.1 IoT and WFH

IoT essentially consists of four components: sensors, networks, cloud, and applications (SNCA), and COVID-19 pushed their adoption and implementation to the max with the sudden pivot of many companies to work from home (WFH) option. Even before the pandemic, the IoT technologies that were of most interests to companies were sensors (84%), data processing (77%), and cloud platforms (76%). Remote working has been the standard for many companies for the last few months and will continue to be so wherever possible. It offers more flexibility, less time wasted on home-work trips, and it allows companies to save on physical spaces and to have teams working in different locations. IoT-connected devices will make it a more appealing and easy option for many organizations [181] Figure 33.1.

33.2 IoT and Blockchain

With blockchain, we can share any transaction/information, in real time, between relevant parties present as nodes in the chain in a secure and immutable fashion. In this case, had there been a blockchain network where WHO, Health Ministry of each country, and maybe even relevant nodal hospitals of each country were connected, sharing real-time information, about any new communicable disease, then the world might have woken up much earlier. We might have seen travel restrictions given sooner, quarantining policies set sooner, and social distancing implemented faster. And maybe fewer countries would have got impacted.

What every country is doing now fighting this pandemic would have been restricted to fewer countries and on a much smaller scale. The usage of a blockchain to share the information early on might have saved the world a lot of pain and deaths. This is an area where IoT and blockchain converged, with all the info. Coming from the sensors/nodes and traveling over available networks to be processed in the cloud and presented via applications in the hands of health workers and authorities, blockchain will secure the data all the way [182].

33.3 IoT and E-Commerce

With the disruption of supply chain networks because of COVID-19, inventory control was one of the biggest challenges retailers and wholesalers had to face during lockdown – and this difficulty may continue until the end of the year. But, indisputably, companies that were already using NFC labels, for example, to control inventory in and out of warehouses have had this task made easier. On the other hand, the track and trace systems used by some carrier companies have proved essential to keep the e-commerce in full operation and to manage the delays in deliveries in real time. In other words, IoT has become a way to offer a faster and more transparent service to the final consumer. If the containment changes our consumption habits, this could be one of the new demands.

33.4 IoT and Telemedicine

COVID-19 pandemic will kickstart IoT adoption in many sectors but especially in the healthcare sector, keeping in mind the strain on healthcare systems caused by the crisis has brought into focus the potential efficiency benefits that can be gained from remote monitoring in healthcare. The sector has been historically slow to integrate IoT technologies into its ecosystem; however, current researches anticipate that the continuing pandemic will drive the adoption of remote monitoring to minimize public interactions [180].

The healthcare institutes in the world are facing difficulties in providing medical care and reducing the risk of exposure. Emphasis on contactless medical care drives the healthcare centers to look up to the IoT solution providers for an effective approach to tackle diseases.

The Internet of Medical Things (IoMT) along with cloud technologies and AI offer an opportunity to help healthcare professionals to monitor their patients, access the data, and provide treatment from a remote location; this is possible by using devices like smart thermometers, smart wearables, track and trace apps, robots, and smart medical devices [181].

References

[180] https://futureiot.tech/analysts-say-covid-19-pandemic-will-spur-iot-adoption/
[181] https://blog.infraspeak.com/iot-covid-19/
[182] https://www.bbvaopenmind.com/en/technology/digital-world/blockchain-technology-and-covid-19/

34

IoT and 5G Convergence

The convergence of *5G* and Internet of Things (*IoT*) is the next natural move for two advance technologies built to make users live conveniently, easier, and more productive. But before talking about how they will unite, we need to understand each of the two technologies.

Simply defined, 5G is the next-generation cellular network compared to 4G, the current standard, which offers speeds ranging from 7 to 17 Mbps for upload and from 12 to 36 Mbps for download; 5G transmission speeds may be as high as 20 Gbps. Latency will also be close to 10% of 4G transmission, and the number of devices that can be connected scales up significantly which warranted the convergence with IoT [183].

The Internet of Things (IoT) is an ecosystem of ever-increasing complexity; a universe of connected things providing key physical data and further

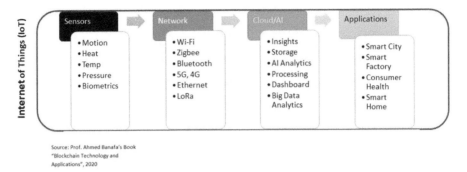

Figure 34.1   Components of IoT.

processing of that data in the cloud to deliver business insights – presents a huge opportunity for many players in all businesses and industries. Many companies are organizing themselves to focus on IoT and the connectivity of their future products and services. IoT can be better understood by its four components: sensors, networks, cloud/AI, and applications as shown in Figure 34.1 [184, 185, 191].

When you combine both technologies, 5G will hit all components of IoT directly or indirectly, sensors will have more bandwidth to report actions, and networks will deliver more information faster. For cloud and AI, the case of real-time data will be used for data analysis and extracting insights, and applications will have more features and cover many options, given the wide bandwidth provided by 5G.

34.1 Benefits of using 5G in IoT

34.1.1 Higher transmission speed

With transmission's speed that can reach 15–20 Gbps, we can access data, files, and programs on remote applications much faster. By increasing the usage of the cloud and making all devices depend less on the internal memory of the device, it will not be necessary to install numerous processors on a device because computing can be done on the cloud. This will increase the longevity of sensors and open the door for more types of sensors with different types of data including high-definition images and real-time motion to list a few [186].

34.1.2 More devices connected

5G impact on IoT is clearly the increased number of devices that can be connected to the network. All connected devices are able to communicate with each other in real time and exchange information. For example, smart homes will have hundreds of devices connected in every possible way to make our life more convenient and enjoyable with smart appliances, energy, and security and entertainment devices. In the case of industrial plants, we are talking about thousands of connected devices used for streamlining the manufacturing process and provide safety and security; in addition to the concept of building a smart [186].

34.1.3 Lower latency

In simple words, latency is the time that passes between the order given to your smart device till the action occurs. Thanks to 5G, this time will be ten times less than what it was in 4G. For example, due to lower latency, the use of sensors can be increased in industrial plants, including control of machinery, control over logistics, or remote transport. Another example, lower latency led healthcare professionals to intervene in surgical operations from remote areas with the help of precision instrumentation that can be managed remotely [186].

34.2 Challenges Faced by 5G and IoT Convergence

34.2.1 Operating across multiple spectrum bands

5G will not replace all the existing cellular technologies any time soon; it is going to be an option besides what we have now, and also new hardware needed to take full advantage of the power of 5G, IoT's second component "networks" will have more options now and can deal with a wide spectrum of frequencies as needed, instead of being limited to few options [185, 187].

34.2.2 A gradual upgradation from 4G to 5G

The plan is to replace 4G in a gradual way with all the infrastructure available now, and this must be done on multiple levels and phases: software, hardware, and access points. This needs big investment by both sides' users and businesses, and different parts of the nation will have different timelines to replace 4G and that will create challenges in the services provided based on 5G. In addition, the ability and desire of users to upgrade their devices to a "5G compatible" device is still a big unknown; a lot of incentives and education are needed to convince individuals and businesses to make the move [187, 189].

34.2.3 Data interoperability

This is an issue on the side of IoT; as the industry evolves, the need for a standard model to perform common IoT backend tasks, such as processing, storage, and firmware updates, is becoming more relevant. In that new sought model, we are likely to see different IoT solutions work with common backend services, which will guarantee levels of interoperability, portability, and manageability that are almost impossible to achieve with the current generation of IoT solutions. Creating that model will never be an easy task by any level of imagination; there are hurdles and challenges facing the standardization and implementation of IoT solutions, and that model needs to overcome all of them. Interoperability is one of the major challenges [188].

34.2.4 Establishing 5G business models

The bottom line is a big motivation for starting, investing in, and operating any business. Without a sound and solid business model for 5G-IoT convergence, we will have another bubble; this model must satisfy all the requirements for all kinds of e-commerce: vertical markets, horizontal markets, and consumer markets. But this category is always a victim of regulatory and legal scrutiny [188].

34.3 Examples of Applications of 5G in IoT

34.3.1 Automotive

One of the primary use cases of 5G is the concept of connected cars, enhanced vehicular communications services which include both direct communication (between vehicles, vehicle to pedestrian, and vehicle to infrastructure) and network-facilitated communication for autonomous driving. In addition to this, use cases supported will focus on vehicle convenience and safety, including intent sharing, path planning, coordinated driving, and real-time local updates. This bring us to the concept of edge computing which is a promising derivative of cloud computing, where edge computing allows computing, decision-making, and action-taking to happen via IoT devices and only pushes relevant data to the cloud; these devices, called edge nodes, can be deployed anywhere with a network connection: on a factory floor, on top of a power pole, alongside a railway track, in a vehicle, or on an oil rig. Any device with computing, storage, and network connectivity can be an edge node. Examples include industrial controllers, switches, routers, embedded servers, and video surveillance cameras. 5G will make communications between edge devices and cloud a breeze [187, 189].

34.3.2 Industrial

The Industrial Internet of Things (IIoT) is a network of physical objects, systems, platforms, and applications that contain embedded technology to communicate and share intelligence with each other, the external environment, and with people. The adoption of the IIoT is being enabled by the improved availability and affordability of sensors, processors, and other technologies that have helped facilitate capture of and access to real-time information. 5G will not only offer a more reliable network but would also deliver an extremely secure network for industrial IoT by integrating security into the core network architecture. Industrial facilities will be among the major users of *private* 5G networks [187, 190].

34.3.3 Healthcare

The requirement for real-time networks will be achieved using 5G, which will significantly transform the healthcare industry. Use cases include live transmission of high-definition surgery videos that can be remotely monitored. The concept of telemedicine with real-time and bigger bandwidth will be a reality. IoT's sensors will be more sophisticated to give more in-depth medical information of patients on the fly; for example, a doctor can check up and diagnose patients while they are on the emergency vehicle on the way to the hospital saving minutes which can be the difference between life and death. The 2020 pandemic taught us the significance of alternative channels of seeing our doctor beside in person, and many startups created apps for telemedicine services during that period. 5G will propel the use of such apps and make our doctor visits more efficient and less time-consuming [187].

References

[183] https://davra.com/5g-internet-of-things/
[184] https://www.linkedin.com/pulse/iot-blockchain-challenges-risks-ahmed-banafa/
[185] https://www.linkedin.com/pulse/three-major-challenges-facing-iot-ahmed-banafa/
[186] https://appinventiv.com/blog/5g-and-iot-technology-use-cases/

[187] https://www.geospatialworld.net/blogs/how-5g-plays-important-role-in-internet-of-things/

[188] https://www.linkedin.com/pulse/iot-standardization-implementation-challenges-ahmed-banafa/

[189] https://www.linkedin.com/pulse/why-iot-needs-fog-computing-ahmed-banafa/

[190] https://www.linkedin.com/pulse/industrial-internet-things-iiot-challenges-benefits-ahmed-banafa/

[191] https://www.amazon.com/Secure-Smart-Internet-Things-IoT/dp/8770220301/

PART 8

Wearable and Mobile Technology

35

The Smart Platform: Wearable Computing Devices (WCD)

Wearable computing devices (WCD): Refers to computer-powered devices or equipment that can be worn by a user, including clothing, watches, glasses, shoes, and similar items.

Wearable computing devices can range from providing very specific, limited features like heart rate monitoring and pedometer capabilities to advanced "smart" functions and features similar to those a smartphone or smartwatch offers. More advanced wearable computing devices can typically enable the user to take and view pictures or video, read text messages and emails, respond to voice commands, browse the web, and more [192].

So far, a shortage of apps has been a major shortfall of many wearable devices. Some smart watches might have only 15–20 apps, and they often need Bluetooth to connect to a nearby smartphone. Compare that number to a million-plus apps in Apple's App Store or Google Play for smartphones.

Analysts expect not only an explosion of wearable computing devices in the next three years but also a big wave of mobile apps of all kinds. Research firm *Gartner* predicted last year that wearable devices will drive half of all app interactions.

35.1 Concerns with Wearable Computing Devices

- *Privacy* concerns over devices that continuously gather and log visual and other data

- Technological *dependence* created by augmented reality and automatic processing

- Power management and heat dissipation

- Software architectures and interfaces

- Management of wireless and personal area networks (PANs)

- Security

35.2 Applications of Wearable Computing Devices

The hands-free and location-independent operations of WCD could have a number of applications.

For example, WCD used by those needing high-tech mobility and connectivity in the field, such as emergency personnel, search-and-rescue teams, warehouse workers, or anyone on the move. WCD also makes it possible to track individuals, such as nurses performing rounds or emergency workers in the field. WCD could display schematics to a technician repairing a specialized piece of machinery. Wearable computing devices could also manage equipment remotely, such as assembly-line machinery, providing an extra layer of *safety* for the worker. Sales personnel could take advantage of easily accessible information to deliver better and faster customer service [193].

35.3 The Future of Wearable Computing Devices

Wearable tech is obviously a hugely exciting concept far from being just a dream; there are many products being produced right now which could easily be placed in that category. Some already have been released, though in limited numbers for the most part. While wearable tech will not be replacing smartphones any time soon, and likely will not be widely used for years to come, the future is bright for this exciting industry. There was a time when cell phones were rare and their usage seemed strange and disagreeable to some. That time has obviously passed us by. Wearable tech will go through the same process. At first, it will seem strange and perhaps a little scary, but as time continues on, these products will almost certainly become hugely popular. *They have too much potential to be ignored.* If the evolution of smartphones and tablets is any indication of the future of wearable computing devices, it is safe to assume that anything is possible [194].

References

[192] http://www.computerworld.com/s/article/9245632/As_wearable_devices_hit_the_market_apps_are_sure_to_follow
[193] http://www.neongoldfish.com/blog/social-media/the-advantages-and-disadvantages-of-wearable-tech/#sthash.eij8N9WN.dpuf
[194] http://searchconsumerization.techtarget.com/opinion/Wearable-computing-devices-could-have-enterprise-prospects

36

Your Smart Device Will Feel Your Pain and Fear

What if your smart device could empathize with you? The evolving field known as *affective computing* is likely to make it happen soon. Scientists and engineers are developing systems and devices that can recognize, interpret, process, and simulate human affects or emotions. It is an interdisciplinary field spanning computer science, psychology, and cognitive science. While its origins can be traced to longstanding philosophical enquiries into emotion, a 1995 paper on affective computing by Rosalind Picard catalyzed modern progress [195].

The more smart devices we have in our lives, the more we are going to want them to behave politely and be socially smart. We do not want them to bother us with unimportant information or overload us with too much information. That kind of common-sense reasoning requires an understanding of our emotional state. We are starting to see such systems perform specific, predefined functions, like changing in real time how you are presented with the questions in a quiz or recommending a set of videos in an educational program to fit the changing mood of students.

How can we make a device that responds appropriately to your emotional state? Researchers are using sensors, microphones, and cameras combined with software logic. A device with the ability to detect and appropriately respond to a user's emotions and other stimuli could gather cues from a variety of sources. Facial expressions, posture, gestures, speech, the force or rhythm of key strokes, and the temperature changes of a hand on a mouse can all potentially signify emotional changes that can be detected and interpreted by a computer. A built-in camera, for example, may capture images of a user. Speech, gesture, and facial recognition technologies are being explored for affective computing applications [196].

Just looking at speech alone, a computer can observe innumerable variables that may indicate emotional reaction and variation. Among these are a person's rate of speaking, accent, pitch, pitch range, final lowering, stress frequency, breathiness, brilliance, loudness, and discontinuities in the pattern of pauses or pitch.

Gestures can also be used to detect emotional states, especially when used in conjunction with speech and face recognition. Such gestures might include simple reflexive responses, like lifting your shoulders when you do not know the answer to a question. Or they could be complex and meaningful, as when communicating with sign language.

A third approach is the monitoring of physiological signs. These might include pulse and heart rate or minute contractions of facial muscles. Pulses in blood volume can be monitored, as can what is known as galvanic skin response. This area of research is still relatively new, but it is gaining momentum and we are starting to see real products that implement the techniques.

Recognizing emotional information requires the extraction of meaningful patterns from the gathered data. Some researchers are using machine learning techniques to detect such patterns.

Detecting emotion in people is one thing. But work is also going into computers that themselves show what appear to be emotions. Already in use are systems that simulate emotions in automated telephone and online conversation agents to facilitate interactivity between human and machine.

There are many applications for affective computing. One is in education. Such systems can help address one of the major drawbacks of online learning versus in-classroom learning: the difficulty faced by teachers in adapting pedagogical situations to the emotional state of students in the classroom. In e-learning applications, affective computing can adjust the presentation style of a computerized tutor when a learner is bored, interested, frustrated, or pleased. Psychological health services also benefit from affective computing applications that can determine a client's emotional state.

Robotic systems capable of processing affective information can offer more functionality alongside human workers in uncertain or complex environments. Companion devices, such as digital pets, can use affective computing abilities to enhance realism and display a higher degree of autonomy.

Other potential applications can be found in social monitoring. For example, a car might monitor the emotion of all occupants and invoke additional safety measures, potentially alerting other vehicles if it detects the driver to be angry. Affective computing has potential applications in human–computer interaction, such as affective "mirrors" that allow the user to see how he or she performs. One example might be warning signals that tell a driver if they are sleepy or going too fast or too slow. A system might even call relatives if the driver is sick or drunk (though one can imagine mixed reactions on the part of the driver to such developments). Emotion-monitoring agents might issue a warning before one sends an angry email, or a music player could select tracks based on your mood. Companies may even be able to use affective computing to infer whether their products will be well-received by the market by detecting facial or speech changes in potential customers when they read an ad or first use the product. Affective computing is also starting to be applied to the development of communicative technologies for use by people with autism.

Many universities have done extensive work on affective computing; resulting projects include something called the galvactivator which was a good starting point. It is a glove-like wearable device that senses a wearer's skin conductivity and maps values to a bright LED display. Increases in skin conductivity across the palm tend to indicate physiological arousal; so the display glows brightly. This may have many potentially useful purposes, including self-feedback for stress management, facilitation of conversation between two people, or visualizing aspects of attention while learning. Along with the revolution in wearable computing technology, affective computing is poised to become more widely accepted, and there will be endless applications for affective computing in many aspects of life.

One of the future applications will be the use of affective computing in metaverse applications, which will humanize the avatar and add emotion as fifth dimension opening limitless possibilities, but all these advancements in applications of affective computing racing to make the machines more human will come with challenges namely SSP (security, safety, and privacy), the three pillars of online user; we need to make sure all the three pillars of online user are protected and well defined. It is easier said than done, but clear guidelines of what, where, and who will use the data will make acceptance of hardware and software of affective computing faster without replacing physical pain with mental pain of fear of privacy and security and safety of our data [197].

References

[195] https://www.linkedin.com/pulse/20140424221437-246665791-affective-computing/
[196] https://www.linkedin.com/pulse/20140730042327-246665791-your-computer-will-feel-your-pain/
[197] https://explorerresearch.com/gsr-market-research/

37

Technology Under Your Skin: Three Challenges of Microchip Implants

Technology continues to get closer to merge with our bodies, from the smartphones in our hands to the smartwatches on our wrists to earbuds. Now, it is getting under our skin literally with a tiny microchip. A *human microchip implant* is typically an identifying integrated circuit device or radio-frequency identification (RFID) transponder encased in silicate glass and implanted in the body of a human being. This type of subdermal implant usually contains a unique ID number that can be linked to information contained in an external database, such as personal identification, law enforcement, medical history, medications, allergies, and contact information [203].

In Sweden, thousands have had microchips inserted into their hands. The chips are designed to speed up users' daily routines and make their lives more convenient – accessing their homes, offices, and gyms is as easy as swiping their hands against digital readers. Chips also can be used to store emergency contact details, social media profiles, or e-tickets for events and rail journeys [199].

Advocates of the tiny chips say that they are safe and largely protected from hacking, but scientists are raising privacy concerns around the kind of personal health data that might be stored on the devices. Around the size of a grain of rice, the chips typically are inserted into the skin just above each user's thumb, using a syringe similar to that used for giving vaccinations. Implanting chips in humans has privacy and security implications that go well beyond cameras in public places, facial recognition, tracking of our locations, our driving habits, our spending histories, and even beyond ownership of your data, which poses great challenges for the acceptance of this technology [198, 199].

To understand the big picture about this technology, you need to know that the use of the chips is an extension of the concept of Internet of Things (IoT), which is a universe of connected things that keep growing by the minute with over 30 billion connected devices at the end of 2020 and 75 billion devices by 2025. Just as the world begins to understand the many benefits of the Internet of Things, but also learns about the "dark side" from "smart everything," including our connected cities, we are now looking at small chips causing major new privacy challenges [198, 202, 204].

Like any new trend, in order for that trend to be accepted and become main stream, it needs to overcome three challenges: *technology, business, and society (regulations and laws)* Figure 37.1.

The first challenge is technology: which is advancing every day and the chips are getting smaller and smarter; in the world of IoT, the chips are considered as the first element of a typical IoT system which consists of sensors, networks, cloud, and applications. As a sensor, the chip touches upon your hand, your heart, your brain, and the rest of your body – literally. This new development is set to give a very different meaning to "hacking the body" or biohacking. While cyber experts continue to worry about protecting critical infrastructure and mitigating security risks that could harm the economy or cause a loss of life, implanted chips also affect health but add in new dimensions to the risks and threats of hacking of sensors as they are considered as the weakest link in IoT systems [198].

The second challenge is business: there are many companies in this field and the opportunities are huge with all aspects of replacing ID in stores, offices, airports, and hospitals, just to mention a few. Also, chips will provide key physical data and further processing of that data in the cloud to deliver business insights, new treatments, and better services – presents a huge opportunity for many players in all types of businesses and industries in private and public sectors [202].

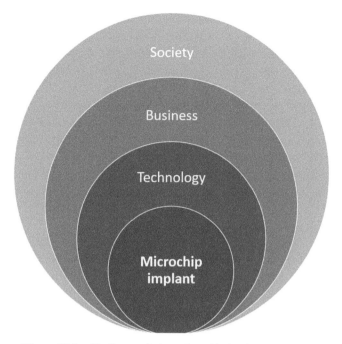

Figure 37.1   Challenges facing microchip implant technology.

The third challenge is society: as individuals try to grapple with the privacy and security implications that come with technologies like IoT, big data, public- and private-sector data breaches, social media sharing, GDPR, a new California privacy law CCPA, along with data ownership and "right to be forgotten" provisions, along comes a set of technologies that will become much more personal than your smartphone or cloud storage history, and the tiny chip under your skin is sitting at the top of the list of these technologies, posing new risks and threats [198].

This challenge can be divided into two tracks: government regulations like GDPR in EU and recent regulations in the US to ban forced usage of the chip, for example, and consumer trust which is built on three pillars: security, safety, and privacy (SSP).

Safety is a major concern in using tiny chips inside your body including infection risks, MRI's use with chips, and corrosion of the chip's parts.

Security and privacy concerns deal with stolen identity, risk to human freedom, and autonomy to mention a few [203].

This technology is promising and it's another step toward more convenience and simplifying many of the daily tasks of billions of people around the world, but without solid security, safety and privacy measures applied when using this tiny chip, we will be facing a cybersecurity nightmare with far reaching consequences, in addition to an ethical dilemma in dealing with population who refused to use it is, they will be marginalized when it comes to jobs for instance. According to a recent survey of employees in the United States and Europe, two-thirds of employees believe that in 2035, humans with chips implanted in their bodies will have an unfair advantage in the labor market. One big concern raised by many privacy advocates is the creation of surveillance state tracking individual using this technology [200].

Too many moving parts to deal with, in this technology, until we answer all questions related to this technology, many people will look at it as another attempt of both governments and businesses to gain access to another piece of data about us and add it to many channels used now in gathering info. Using our electronic devices, knowing that by 2030, there will be an average of 15 IoT devices for each person in the US [204].

References

[198] https://www.govtech.com/blogs/lohrmann-on-cybersecurity/chip-implants-the-next-big-privacy-debate.html
[199] https://www.npr.org/2018/10/22/658808705/thousands-of-swedes-are-inserting-microchips-under-their-skin
[200] https://www.cnn.com/2020/09/18/business/jobs-robots-microchips-cyborg/index.html
[201] https://www.thomasnet.com/insights/the-future-of-microchip-implants-in-humans/
[202] https://www.linkedin.com/pulse/three-major-challenges-facing-iot-ahmed-banafa/
[203] https://en.wikipedia.org/wiki/Microchip_implant_(human)
[204] https://www.linkedin.com/pulse/8-key-tech-trends-post-covid-19-world-ahmed-banafa/

PART 9

Future Trends in Technology

38

The Metaverse: A Different Perspective

The term "metaverse" is a hot topic of conversation recently, with many tech giants like Facebook and Microsoft staking claims. But what is the metaverse?

Author Neal Stephenson is credited with coining the term "metaverse" in his 1992 science fiction novel "Snow Crash," in which he envisioned lifelike avatars who met in realistic 3D buildings and other virtual reality environments. Similarly, metaverse in a technical sense is another name of Internet of Everything (IoE), a concept started in the early 2000s which led to Internet of Things and its applications, a scale down version of IoE [205].

Since then, various developments have made mileposts on the way toward a real metaverse, an online virtual world which incorporates augmented reality (AR), virtual reality (VR), 3D holographic avatars, video, and other means of communication. As the metaverse expands, it will offer a hyper-real alternative world. But this description is like talking about "Frontend" in apps development without explaining the "Backend" side of the apps. To understand that side of this new Xverse, we need to look at metaverse from a different perspective [206].

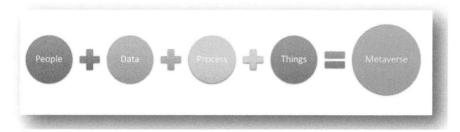

Figure 38.1   Components of the metaverse.

38.1 Different Perspective of the Metaverse

The *"metaverse" is bringing together people, process, data, and things (real and virtual) to make networked connections more relevant and valuable than ever before-turning information into actions that create new capabilities, richer experiences, and unprecedented economic opportunity for businesses, individuals, and countries"* Figure 38.1.

In simple terms, metaverse is the intelligent connection of people, process, data, and things. The metaverse describes a world where billions of objects have sensors to detect measure and assess their status; all connected over public or private networks using standard and proprietary protocols [207].

38.2 Pillars of the Metaverse

- *People*: Connecting people in more relevant, valuable ways

- *Data*: Converting data into intelligence to make better decisions

- *Process*: Delivering the right information to the right person (or machine) at the right time

- *Things*: Physical and virtual devices and objects connected to the internet and each other for intelligent decision making.

38.3 The Future

Data is embedded in everything we do; every business needs its own flavor of data strategy which requires a comprehensive data leadership. The metaverse will create tens of millions of new objects and sensors, all generating real-time data which will add more value to their products and services for all the companies who will use metaverse as another avenue of business. Enterprises will make extensive use of metaverse technology, and there will be a wide range of products sold into various markets vertical and horizontal, an endless list of products and services [208].

For example, in e-commerce, the metaverse provides a whole new revenue stream for digital goods in a synchronic way instead of the current traditional way of click and buy. In human resources (HR), significant training resources will be done with virtual reality (VR) and augmented reality (AR) that are overlaying instructions in a real-world environment and giving somebody a step-by-step playbook on how to put complex machine together or run a device or try a new product, all will be done with virtual objects at the heart of the metaverse. While in sales/marketing, connecting with customers virtually and sharing virtual experience of the product or service will be common similar to our virtual meetings during the past two years in the middle of Covid, but the metaverse will make it more real and more productive [209].

Crypto products including NFTs will be the natives of the metaverse adding another block to Web 3.0 Xverse.

But as devices/people get more connected and collect more data and the metaverse is expanded at a speed higher than the speed of the real universe, privacy and security concerns will increase too. How companies decide to balance customer privacy with this wealth of metaverse data will be critical for the future of the metaverse and, more importantly, customers' trust of the metaverse and any future Xverse versions [210].

References

[205] https://cointelegraph.com/news/new-tribes-of-the-metaverse-community-owned-economies
[206] https://biv.com/article/2021/11/top-business-applications-metaverse
[207] https://www.usatoday.com/story/tech/2021/11/10/metaverse-what-is-it-explained-facebook-microsoft-meta-vr/6337635001/
[208] http://www.cisco.com/web/about/ac79/innov/IoE.html
[209] http://internetofeverything.cisco.com/
[210] http://www.cisco.com/web/solutions/trends/iot/overview.html

39

The Metaverse: Myths and Facts

Any new technology involves a certain amount of ambiguity and myths. In the case of the metaverse, however, many of the myths have been exaggerated and facts were misrepresented; while the metaverse vision will take years to mature fully, the building blocks to begin this process are already in place. Key hardware and software are either available today or under development; definitely, stakeholders need to address safety, security, and privacy (SSP) concerns and collaborate to implement open standards that will make the metaverse safe, secure, reliable, and interoperable and allow the delivery of secured and safe services as seamlessly as possible.

Despite the buzz about the metaverse, many still do not completely understand it. For some, it is the future, while others think it is gimmicky. For now, the metaverse is an interface or a platform that allows digital realities of people to come together to work, play, and collaborate. Metaverse hopes to transcend geographical boundaries and become the next "thing." That being said, there are plenty of misconceptions about the metaverse, and here are a few [216].

39.1 Myths about the Metaverse

39.1.1 Myth #1: No one knows what the metaverse is

In recent months, it has become clear that there is no single definition of the metaverse. Well-known experts refer to it as "the internet of the future" or point to immersive devices to demonstrate various platforms and user experiences [212].

In simple terms, the metaverse is the future of the internet: a massively scaled, interactive, and interoperable real-time platform comprising interconnected virtual worlds where people can socialize, collaborate, transact, play, and create. There are 5 billion internet users in the world and crypto has emerged as both the infrastructure layer and the zeitgeist that will fill in the blanks: digital currency, fully functioning digital economies, ownership of digital goods, and true interoperability across countless interconnected systems, all this defines the metaverse [213].

39.1.2 Myth #2: The metaverse is only gaming

The metaverse is not gaming. Gaming is an activity you can do within the metaverse; there are 3 billion gamers in the world. Today, when people talk about the metaverse, they often describe gaming platforms like *Roblox* and *Minecraft* as examples. While gaming remains one of the leading experiences, consumers are increasingly looking for entertainment and shopping in the virtual world. One in five metaverse users has attended virtual live events such as concerts and film festivals [214].

39.1.3 Myth #3: The metaverse is only virtual reality

Saying the metaverse is virtual reality (VR) is like saying that the internet is only your smartphone; it is a way of interfacing with the internet. In the same way, you can imagine experiencing the metaverse through VR, but you can also imagine experiencing the metaverse through your laptop or desktop [214].

39.1.4 Myth #4: The metaverse will replace the real world

No, this is not the "Matrix"; the metaverse will not replace the real world. It will be additive to the real world, an expansive virtual environment where you

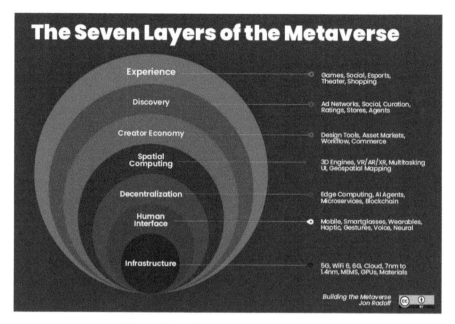

Figure 39.1   Seven layers of the metaverse.

can do any number of different things: work, socialize, play, create, explore, and more [214] Figure 39.1.

39.1.5 Myth #5: The metaverse is a fad

The metaverse is a fad in the same way the internet considered as a fad at some point of time. We are still years away from a fully realized metaverse, and the technology we will need is far from complete. But even today, we are already living in a very primitive version: we work remotely, we socialize and learn virtually, and we find entertainment without leaving our homes. However, as always, how we meet those needs will continue to evolve as our technology advances [214].

39.1.6 Myth #6: The metaverse will be a monopoly

Companies like Meta and Microsoft are two of the world's most valuable companies because they are perceptive. They have a skill for skating to where the puck will be and they are able to scale fast. But jumping on the band-wagon early does not mean they will control the metaverse; the field is too big to be controlled by handful companies [214].

39.1.7 Myth #7: The speed of technology will set the pace for adoption

Many people believe that the broad adoption of the metaverse is hindered because technology is not keeping pace. There remains low penetration of immersive devices among consumers, and there are infrastructure barriers in the way of a truly scaled, immersive metaverse future. Close to one-third of metaverse users see technology as severely limiting their dream experience.

VR is the most accessible technology at just 20% penetration; yet, the adoption curve to date follows the trajectory of other technologies that became widely available over time. Penetration for recent breakthroughs such as smartphones, tablets, and social media grew from 20% to 50% in only a handful of years. Lower cost, increasing content, and improved usability are driving adoption [214].

39.1.8 Myth #8: The metaverse is already here

The metaverse is an infinitely large (future) virtual world that connects all other virtual sub-worlds. You can see the metaverse as the next phase of the internet as we know it: the currently two-dimensional, flat internet will be changing into a three-dimensional, spatial form. We are moving from the web of pages to the web of coordinates, and from the web of information to the web of activities. In the future, people can meet as avatars in the metaverse, to get to know each other for example, to network, provide services, collaborate, relax, game, shop, and consume. The metaverse also offers the opportunity to build, create, and participate in a virtual economy. In the future, we will not be going "on" the internet, but *"in"* the spatial internet. The metaverse can be seen as the world that connects all (existing) virtual worlds. That world, however, is not here yet; *the* metaverse is still a thing of the future [215].

39.1.9 Myth #9: The metaverse is inevitable

It is clear that the metaverse is actively being developed. The key players in the world of technology have their eyes on it. But they are facing a number of challenges; interoperability for example – where users must be able to move easily between different worlds – being one of them. This means that companies must work intensively on open standards. In the metaverse, you have to be able to work, attend concerts, and play games with the greatest of ease. Not such an easy feat, particularly because many companies will be reluctant to collaborate on open standards and give up their intellectual property. In addition, the growth of the metaverse will also require substantial hardware innovations [215].

39.1.10 Myth #10: The metaverse is suitable for everything

This is another aspect that remains to be seen. In the future, the different variants of the internet will simply coexist – just as you sometimes read a book on paper, and sometimes on your screen. The internet as we know it will continue to exist. It will be accessible on your smartphone, computer, or tablet. For some things such as shopping, playing games, and social interaction, the metaverse will be extremely suitable [215].

39.2 What is the Future of the Metaverse?

The metaverse "is bringing together people, processes, data, and things (real and virtual) to make networked connections more relevant and valuable than ever before-turning information into actions that create new capabilities, richer experiences, and unprecedented economic opportunity for businesses, individuals, and countries." In simple terms, the metaverse is the intelligent connection of people, processes, data, and things. It describes a world where billions of objects have sensors to detect, measure, and assess their status, all connected over public or private networks using standard and proprietary protocols [211].

Data is embedded in everything we do; every business needs its flavor of data strategy, which requires comprehensive data leadership. The metaverse will create tens of millions of new objects and sensors, all generating real-time data which will add more value to their products and services for all the companies who will use metaverse as another avenue of business. As a result, enterprises will make extensive use of metaverse technology. As a result, there will be a wide range of products sold into various markets, vertical and horizontal, an endless list of products and services.

For example, in e-commerce, the metaverse provides a whole new revenue stream for digital goods in a synchronous way instead of the current traditional 2D way of clicking and buying. In human resources (HR), significant training resources will be done with virtual reality (VR) and augmented reality (AR) that are overlaying instructions in a real-world environment and giving somebody a step-by-step playbook on how to put a complex machine together or run a device or try a new product; all will be done with virtual objects at the heart of the metaverse. While in sales/marketing, connecting with customers virtually and sharing the virtual experience of the product or service will be common similar to our virtual meetings during the past two years in the middle of Covid, but the metaverse will make it more real and more productive.

Finally, similarly to cloud computing, we will have private-metaverse, hybrid-metaverse, and public-metaverse with all possible applications and services in each type. Companies will benefit from all options based on their capabilities and needs. The main goal here is to reach metaverse as a service (MaaS) and add a label of "Metaverse Certified" on products and services [211].

References

[211] https://www.bbntimes.com/science/the-Metaverse-a-different-perspective
[212] https://www.mckinsey.com/industries/retail/our-insights/probing-reality-and-myth-in-the-Metaverse
[213] https://venturebeat.com/2022/03/24/5-common-Metaverse-misconceptions/
[214] https://www.mckinsey.com/industries/retail/our-insights/probing-reality-and-myth-in-the-Metaverse
[215] https://jarnoduursma.com/blog/7-misconceptions-about-the-Metaverse/
[216] https://analyticsindiamag.com/misconceptions-about-Metaverse-mark-zuckerberg-virtual-reality-augmented-real-world-gaming/

40

Eight Key Tech Trends in a Post-COVID-19 World

COVID-19 has demonstrated the importance of digital readiness, which allows business and people's life to continue as usual during pandemics. Building the necessary infrastructure to support a digitized world and stay current in the latest technology will be essential for any business or country to remain competitive in a post-COVID-19 world [219].

COVID-19 pandemic is the ultimate catalyst for digital transformation and will greatly accelerate several major trends that were already well underway before the pandemic. The COVID-19 pandemic will have a lasting effect not only on our economy but on how we go about our daily lives, and things are not likely to return to pre-pandemic norms. While this pandemic has forced many businesses to reduce or suspend operations, affecting their bottom line, it has helped to accelerate the development of several emerging technologies. This is especially true for innovations that reduce human-to-human contact, automate processes, and increase productivity amid social distancing [218].

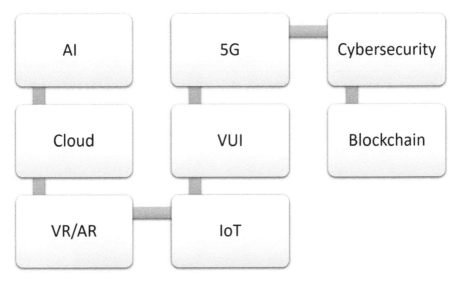

Figure 40.1   Eight key tech trends in a post-COVID-19 world.

The following technologies stand to bourgeon in a post-COVID-19 world Figure 40.1.

40.1 Artificial Intelligence (AI)

By 2030, AI products will contribute more than $15.7 trillion to the global economy. A number of technological innovations such as intelligent data processing, and face and speech recognition have become possible due to AI [219].

Post COVID-19, consumer behaviors will not go back to pre-pandemic norms. Consumers will purchase more goods and services online, and increasing numbers of people will work remotely. As companies begin to navigate the post-COVID-19 world as economies slowly begin to reopen, the application of artificial intelligence (AI) will be extremely valuable in helping them adapt to these new trends [220].

AI will be particularly useful for those within retail and supply chain industries. Through machine learning and advanced data analytics, AI will help these companies detect new purchasing patterns and deliver a greater personalized experience to online customers [218].

AI tools analyze large amounts of data to learn underlying patterns, enabling computer systems to make decisions, predict human behavior, and recognize images and human speech, among many other things. AI-enabled systems also continuously learn and adapt. These capabilities will be extremely valuable as companies confront and adapt to the next normal once this pandemic subsides [218].

AI will increasingly contribute to the forecasting of consumers' behavior, which became hardly predictable, and to help businesses organize effective logistics. Chatbots may provide clients' support 24/7, one of the "must-haves" during the lockdown [219].

40.2 Cloud Computing

Fortunately, cloud companies are weathering the pandemic stress-test caused by the sudden spike in workloads and waves of new, inexperienced users. Microsoft reports a 775% spike in cloud services demand from COVID-19 [222].

In post-COVID-19 world, cloud technology is likely to receive a surge in implementation across all types of apps. As the virus spread, people were forced to work from home (WFH) and online learning models were implemented, and the demand for cloud-based video conferencing and teaching has skyrocketed. Various cloud service vendors have actively upgraded their functions and provided resources to meet this demand. Moving forward, businesses and educational institutions are likely to continue to make use of this technology. As demand for this technology continues to grow, implementation of this technology into mobile applications for easier access will be key, for the cloud the sky is the limit [218].

40.3 VR/AR

This pandemic increased the number of people using VR headsets to play video games, explore virtual travel destinations, and partake in online entertainment; as they isolate at home, they are also using this technology to seek human interaction through social VR platforms.

Businesses have also been experimenting with VR platforms to train employees, hold conferences, collaborate on projects, and connect employees virtually. For example, scientists worldwide have turned to VR platform for molecular design, to collaborate on coronavirus research and potential treatments. Now that businesses and consumers know the extent to which this technology can be used, we are likely to see more virtual conferences and human interactions as our new normal sets in [218].

40.4 5G Networks

5G is acknowledged as the future of communication and the cutting edge for the entire mobile industry. Deployment of 5G networks will emerge between

2020 and 2030, making possible zero-distance connectivity between people and connected machines. This type of mobile internet connectivity will provide us super-fast download and upload speeds (five times faster than 4G capabilities) as well as more stable connections [219].

The industry buzz surrounding 5G technology and its impact on the next-generation of connectivity and services has been circulating over the last year or so. Yet, the technology still is not widely available and it holds the potential to revolutionize the way mobile networks function; because of COVID-19, the 5G market may materialize sooner than expected. As large numbers of people have been forced to isolate, an increase in working and studying from home has been stressing networks and creating higher demand for bandwidth. People have now realized the need for faster data sharing with increased connectivity speeds; an acceleration in the rollout of 5G technology to ensure the bandwidth and capacity challenges of existing infrastructure is more real than ever [217, 218].

40.5 Voice User Interface (VUI)

As consumers are becoming increasingly concerned that their mobile devices (which are touched more than 2600 times per day) can spread coronavirus. As the fear of spreading germs grows, so will the use of voice tech in forms of voice user interface (VUI), which can reduce the number of times one touches any surface, including our mobile devices. Almost 80% of our communications is done using verbal communication; that is why voice usage will continue to increase and extend to other smart-home components implicated as major germ hubs. As more TVs and entertainment components, light switches, appliances, plumbing fixtures, and alarm systems incorporate voice control functionality, there will be less need to touch them.

40.6 Internet of Things (IoT)

IoT will enable us to predict and treat health issues in people even before any symptoms appear, with smart medication containers, IP for every vital part of your body for the doctor to hack. To smart forks that tell us if the food is healthy or not. Personalized approaches concerning prescribing medicines and applying treatments will appear (also referred to as precision medicine). In 2019, there were about 26 billion IoT devices and it is estimated by statista.com that their number will increase to 30.73 billion in 2020 and to 75.44 billion in 2025. The market value is about $150 billion with estimated 15 IoT devices for a person in the US by 2030.

IoT also fuels edge computing; thus, data storage and computation become closer to the points of action, enabling saves in bandwidth and low latency. IoT will transform the user experience profoundly, providing opportunities that were not possible before. Gaining this experience may be forced by the pandemic, when people are spending almost all their time at home. IoT devices that make life quality better and daily life more comfortable can become quite trendy. For example, telemedicine and IoT devices helping to monitor people's health indicators may increase their popularity [219].

40.7 Cybersecurity

Cybersecurity is one of the vital technologies for organizations, especially whose business processes are based on data-driven technologies. Much more attention is being paid to privacy and data protection since the European Union's General Data Protection Regulations (GDRP) has been signed, and recently CCPA in California.

During COVID-19 pandemic lockdown, when thousands of people are forced to work remotely, volumes of private data may become totally vulnerable or at least not protected in a proper way. This emerging challenge may give another incentive to the implementation of cybersecurity practices. Cybercriminals took advantage of the fear factor of this virus to send their own viruses; there are many examples of such activities recently including fake domains of COVID-19, phishing emails promising virus protection kits, and even info about canceled summer Olympic games. In addition, there is an increase in ransomware attacks on health institutions and even hacking of research centers to steal any info about possible vaccine of COVID-19 [219].

40.8 Blockchain Technology

The COVID-19 crisis has revealed a general lack of connectivity and data exchange built into our global supply chains. Future resiliency will depend on building transparent, inter-operable, and connective networks. If there were any lingering doubts over the value of blockchain platforms to improve the transparency of businesses that depend on the seamless integration of disparate networks, COVID-19 has all but wiped them away. We should look at this healthcare crisis as a vital learning curve that can show us how to build transparent, inter-operable, and connective networks. Blockchain is

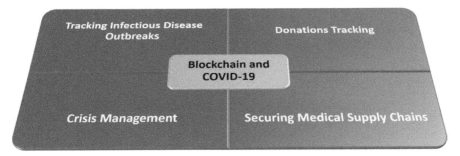

Figure 40.2   Blockchain applications in fighting COVID-19.

supporting efforts around the globe to battle the virus as explained in the following list [220]:

1.   Tracking infectious disease outbreaks

2.   Donations tracking

3.   Crisis management

4.   Securing medical supply chains

40.9 Tracking Infectious Disease Outbreaks

Blockchain can be used for tracking public health data surveillance, particularly for infectious disease outbreaks such as COVID-19. With increased blockchain transparency, it will result in more accurate reporting and efficient responses. Blockchain can help develop treatments swiftly as they would allow for rapid processing of data, thus enabling early detection of symptoms before they spread to the level of epidemics. Additionally, this will enable government agencies to keep track of the virus activity, of patients, suspected new cases, and more [221].

40.10 Donations Tracking

With the help of blockchain capabilities, donors can see where funds are most urgently required and can track their donations until they are provided with a verification that their contributions have been received to the victims. Blockchain would enable transparency for the general public to understand how their donations have been used and its progress [221].

40.11 Crisis Management

Blockchain could also manage crisis situation. It could instantly alert the public about the Coronavirus by global institutes like the World Health Organization (WHO) using *smart contracts* concept. Not only can it alert, but blockchain could also enable to provide governments with recommendations about how to contain the virus. It could offer a secure platform where all the concerning authorities such as governments, medical professionals, media, health organizations, media, and others can update each other about the situation and prevent it from worsening further without censorship [221].

40.12 Securing Medical Supply Chains

Blockchain has already proven its success stories as a supply chain management tool in various industries; similarly, blockchain could also be beneficial in tracking and tracing medical supply chains. Blockchain-based platforms can be useful in reviewing, recording, and tracking of demand, supplies, and logistics of epidemic prevention materials. As supply chains involve multiple parties, the entire process of record and verification is tamper-proof by every party, while also allowing anyone to track the process [221].

References

[217] https://www.weforum.org/agenda/2020/04/10-technology-trends-coronavirus-covid19-pandemic-robotics-telehealth/

[218] https://clearbridgemobile.com/five-emerging-mobile-trends-in-a-post-covid-19-world/

[219] https://www.sharpminds.com/news-entry/the-future-of-it-covid-19-reality-5-technology-trends/

[220] https://www.weforum.org/agenda/2020/05/why-covid-19-makes-a-compelling-case-for-wider-integration-of-blockchain/

[221] https://medium.com/datadriveninvestor/blockchain-technology-and-covid-19-c504fdc775ba

[222] https://www.zdnet.com/article/microsoft-cloud-services-demand-up-775-percent-prioritization-rules-in-place-due-to-covid-19/

References

[1] http://www.fastcolabs.com/3013214/why-quantum-computing-is-faster-for-everything-but-the-web

[2] http://www.theguardian.com/science/2014/mar/06/quantum-computing-explained-particle-mechanics

[3] http://www.economist.com/news/science-and-technology/21578027-first-real-world-contests-between-quantum-computers-and-standard-ones-faster

[4] http://whatis.techtarget.com/definition/quantum-computing

[5] http://physics.about.com/od/quantumphysics/f/quantumcomp.htm

[6] http://www.qi.damtp.cam.ac.uk/node/38

[7] http://www.businessinsider.com/what-is-quantum-encryption-2014-3#ixzz33jYuMw48

[8] http://www.wired.com/2013/06/quantum-cryptography-hack/

[9] http://searchsecurity.techtarget.com/definition/quantum-cryptography

[10] http://science.howstuffworks.com/science-vs-myth/everyday-myths/quantum-cryptology.htm

[11] http://www.wisegeek.com/what-is-quantum-cryptography.htm

[12] http://www.techrepublic.com/blog/it-security/how-quantum-cryptography-works-and-by-the-way-its-breakable/

[13] https://www.cybertalk.org/2020/10/23/quantum-internet-fast-forward-into-the-future/

[14] https://www.bbvaopenmind.com/en/technology/digital-world/quantum-computing/

[15] https://www.zdnet.com/article/what-is-the-quantum-internet-every-thing-you-need-to-know-about-the-weird-future-of-quantum-networks/

[16] https://ahmedbanafa.blogspot.com/2014/06/understanding-quantum-cryptography.html

[17] https://en.wikipedia.org/wiki/Quantum_teleportation

[18] https://www.linkedin.com/pulse/quantum-internet-explained-ahmed-banafa/

[19] https://www.designboom.com/technology/nasa-long-distance-quantum-teleportation-12-22-2020/

[20] https://www.siliconrepublic.com/machines/quantum-computing-fermilab

[21] https://ahmedbanafa.blogspot.com/2019/12/ten-trends-of-iot-in-2020.html

[22] https://ahmedbanafa.blogspot.com/2020/11/quantum-internet-explained.html

[23] https://www.azoquantum.com/Article.aspx?ArticleID=101

[24] https://www.cybersecurityintelligence.com/blog/quantum-computing-the-internet-of-things-and-hackers-4914.html

[25] https://www.europeanbusinessreview.com/iot-security-are-we-ready-for-a-quantum-world/

[26] https://www.bbvaopenmind.com/en/technology/digital-world/quantum-computing-and-blockchain-facts-and-myths/

[27] https://www.ft.com/content/c13dbb51-907b-4db7-8347-30921ef

[28] https://www.forbes.com/sites/billybambrough/2019/10/02/could-google-be-about-to-break-bitcoin/#1d78c5373329

[29] https://decrypt.co/9642/what-google-quantum-computer-means-for-bitcoin/

[30] https://www.coindesk.com/how-should-crypto-prepare-for-googles-quantum-supremacy?

[31] https://www.ccn.com/google-quantum-bitcoin/

[32] https://www.linkedin.com/pulse/20140503185010-246665791-quantum-computing/

[33] https://www.linkedin.com/pulse/20140608053056-246665791-understanding-quantum-

[34] https://www.linkedin.com/pulse/quantum-computing-blockchain-facts-myths-ahmed-banafa/

[35] https://analyticsindiamag.com/will-quantum-computing-define-the-future-of-ai/

[36] https://www.analyticsinsight.net/ai-quantum-computing-can-enable-much-anticipated-advancements/

[37] https://research.aimultiple.com/quantum-ai/

[38] https://www.globenewswire.com/news-release/2020/11/17/2128495/0/en/Quantum-Computing-Market-is-Expected-to-Reach-2-2-Billion-by-2026.html

[39] https://ai.googleblog.com/2019/10/quantum-supremacy-using-programmable.html

[40] https://www.linkedin.com/pulse/quantum-technology-ecosystem-explained-steve-blank/?

[41] https://www.bbvaopenmind.com/en/technology/digital-world/quantum-computing-and-ai/

[42] https://phys.org/news/2022-03-technique-quantum-resilient-noise-boosts.html

[43] https://thequantuminsider.com/2019/10/01/introduction-to-qubits-part-1/

[44] http://www.technologyreview.com/news/524026/is-google-cornering-the-market-on-deep-learning/

[45] http://www.forbes.com/sites/netapp/2013/08/19/what-is-deep-learning/

[46] http://www.fastcolabs.com/3026423/why-google-is-investing-in-deep-learning

[47] http://www.npr.org/blogs/alltechconsidered/2014/02/20/280232074/deep-learning-teaching-computers-to-tell-things-apart

[48] http://www.technologyreview.com/news/519411/facebook-launches-advanced-ai-effort-to-find-meaning-in-your-posts/

[49] http://www.deeplearning.net/tutorial/

[50] http://searchnetworking.techtarget.com/definition/neural-network

[51] https://en.wikipedia.org/wiki/Affective_computing

[52] http://www.gartner.com/it-glossary/affective-computing

[53] http://whatis.techtarget.com/definition/affective-computing

[54] http://curiosity.discovery.com/question/what-is-affective-computing

[55] http://computer.financialexpress.com/20020819/focus1.shtml

[56] http://www.webopedia.com/TERM/A/autonomic_computing.html

[57] http://www.techopedia.com/definition/191/autonomic-computing

[58] http://whatis.techtarget.com/definition/autonomic-computing

[59] https://www.linkedin.com/pulse/8-key-tech-trends-post-covid-19-world-ahmed-banafa/

[60] https://www.bdex.com/thick-data-why-marketers-must-understand-why-people-behave-the-way-they-do/

[61] https://www.usertesting.com/blog/thick-data-vs-big-data

[62] https://www.oracle.com/in/big-data/what-is-big-data/

[63] https://www.cognizant.com/us/en/glossary/thick-data

[64] http://www.brandwatch.com/2014/04/what-is-thick-data-and-why-should-you-use-it/

[65] http://ethnographymatters.net/2013/05/13/big-data-needs-thick-data/

[66] http://www.wired.com/2014/04/your-big-data-is-worthless-if-you-dont-bring-it-into-the-real-world/

[67] http://www.big-dataforum.com/238/big-data-how-about-%E2%80%9Cthick-data%E2%80%9D-%E2%80%94-or-did-we-just-create-another-haystack

[68] http://blog.marketresearch.com/thick-data-and-market-research-understanding-your-customers

[69] http://www.wired.com/2013/03/clive-thompson-2104/

[70] http://h30458.www3.hp.com/us/us/discover-performance/info-management-leaders/2014/jun/tapping-the-profit-potential-of-dark-data.html
[71] http://h30458.www3.hp.com/ww/en/ent/You-have-dark-data_1392257.html
[72] http://www.gartner.com/it-glossary/dark-data
[73] http://www.techopedia.com/definition/29373/dark-data
[74] http://searchdatamanagement.techtarget.com/definition/dark-data
[75] http://www.computerweekly.com/opinion/Dark-data-could-halt-big-datas-path-to-success
[76] http://www.forbes.com/sites/gartnergroup/2014/05/07/digital-business-is-everyones-business/
[77] https://medium.com/what-i-learned-building/7d88d014ba98
[78] http://blogs.pb.com/digital-insights/2014/05/05/dark-data-analytics/
[79] http://blogs.computerworld.com/business-intelligenceanalytics/23286/dark-data-when-it-worth-being-brought-light
[80] http://www.theguardian.com/news/datablog/2013/apr/25/forget-big-data-small-data-revolution
[81] http://whatis.techtarget.com/definition/small-data
[82] http://www.zdnet.com/10-reasons-2014-will-be-the-year-of-small-data-7000023667/
[83] http://www.techopedia.com/definition/29539/small-data
[84] http://technologies.lesechos.fr/partners/capgemini/cacheDirectory/HTMLcontributions/img/20120711152005_BigData.jpeg
[85] http://www.312analytics.com/wp-content/uploads/2013/03/big-data-versus-small-data1.jpg
[86] http://www.b-eye-network.com/blogs/oneal/Big%20data%20Small%20data%20v4.png
[87] https://www.rd-alliance.org/system/files/800px-BigData_SmallData.png
[88] https://www.bmc.com/blogs/data-lake-vs-data-warehouse-vs-database-whats-the-difference/
[89] https://www.guru99.com/data-lake-architecture.html#21
[90] https://www.dataversity.net/data-lakes-what-they-are-and-how-to-use-them/
[91] http://www.gartner.com/newsroom/id/2809117?
[92] http://datascience101.wordpress.com/2014/03/12/what-is-a-data-lake/
[93] http://en.wiktionary.org/wiki/data_lake
[94] http://searchaws.techtarget.com/definition/data-lake
[95] http://www.forbes.com/sites/edddumbill/2014/01/14/the-data-lake-dream/

[96] http://www.platfora.com/wp-content/uploads/2014/06/data-lake.png
[97] http://www.b-eye-network.com/blogs/eckerson/archives/2014/03/beware_of_the_a.php
[98] http://usblogs.pwc.com/emerging-technology/the-future-of-big-data-data-lakes/
[99] http://siliconangle.com/blog/2014/08/07/gartner-drowns-the-concept-of-data-lakes-in-new-report/
[100] http://www.pwc.com/us/en/technology-forecast/2014/issue1/features/data-lakes.jhtml
[101] http://www.ibmbigdatahub.com/blog/don%E2%80%99t-drown-big-data-lake http://www.wallstreetandtech.com/data-management/what-is-a-data-lake/d/d-id/1268851?
[102] http://emcplus.typepad.com/.a/6a0168e71ada4c970c01a3fc-c11630970b-800wi
[103] http://hortonworks.com/wp-content/uploads/2014/05/TeradataHortonworks_Datalake_White-Paper_20140410.pdf
[104] https://www.linkedin.com/pulse/why-iot-needs-fog-computing-ahmed-banafa/
[105] https://www.linkedin.com/pulse/fog-computing-vital-successful-internet-things-iot-ahmed-banafa/
[106] http://www.cisco.com/web/about/ac50/ac207/crc_new/university/RFP/rfp13078.html
[107] http://www.howtogeek.com/185876/what-is-Edge-computing/
[108] http://newsroom.cisco.com/feature-content?type=webcontent&-articleId=1365576
[109] http://www.cisco.com/web/about/ac79/innov/IoE.html
[110] http://internetofeverything.cisco.com/
[111] http://www.cisco.com/web/solutions/trends/iot/overview.html
[112] http://time.com/#539/the-next-big-thing-for-tech-the-internet-of-everything/
[113] http://www.gartner.com/newsroom/id/2621015
[114] http://www.livemint.com/Specials/34DC3bDLSCItBaTfRvMBQO/Internet-of-Everything-gains-momentum.html
[115] http://www.tibco.com/blog/2013/10/07/gartners-internet-of-everything/
[116] http://www.eweek.com/small-business/internet-of-everything-personal-worlds-creating-new-markets-gartner.html
[117] "Secure and Smart IoT" Book, Ahmed Banafa
[118] https://www.linkedin.com/pulse/20140319132744-246665791-the-internet-of-everything-ioe/

[119] http://www.webopedia.com/TERM/C/CDN.html

[120] http://searchaws.techtarget.com/definition/content-delivery-network-CDN

[121] http://en.wikipedia.org/wiki/Content_delivery_network

[122] http://www.akamai.com/html/solutions/sola_cdn.html

[123] http://www.techopedia.com/definition/4191/content-delivery-network-cdn

[124] http://www.pcmag.com/encyclopedia/term/39466/cdn

[125] http://www.6wind.com/software-defined-networking/sdn-nfv-primer/

[126] http://www.tmcnet.com/tmc/whitepapers/documents/whitepapers/2013/9377-network-functions-virtualization-challenges-solutions.pdf

[127] http://www.sdncentral.com/why-sdn-software-defined-networking-or-nfv-network-functions-virtualization-now/

[128] http://www.sdncentral.com/technology/nfv-and-sdn-whats-the-difference/2013/03/

[129] http://www.sdncentral.com/whats-network-functions-virtualization-nfv/

[130] http://www.sdncentral.com/which-is-better-sdn-or-nfv/

[131] http://www.businessnewsdaily.com/5791-virtualization-vs-cloud-computing.html

[132] http://searchservervirtualization.techtarget.com/definition/virtualization

[133] http://www.vmware.com/virtualization

[134] http://www.wisegeek.com/what-are-the-benefits-of-virtualization.htm

[135] http://www.datacenterdynamics.com/focus/archive/2013/10/future-virtualization

[136] http://www.businessnewsdaily.com/5215-dangers-cloud-computing.html

[137] http://www.liquidtechnology.net/blog/cloud-computing-security-risks/

[138] http://www.pwc.com/us/en/issues/cloud-computing/risks.jhtml

[139] http://www.networkworld.com/article/2226230/cisco-subnet/security-professionals-identify-it-risks-associated-with-cloud-computing.html

[140] http://www.infoworld.com/d/security/the-5-cloud-risks-you-have-stop-ignoring-214696?page=0,1

[141] http://www.cloudcomputing-news.net/news/2013/dec/10/ibm-launches-cloud-clouds-offering-aims-stop-vendor-lockin/

[142] http://www.techopedia.com/definition/7756/intercloud

[143] http://www.cloudwards.net/news/ibm-offers-intercloud-storage-2914/

[144] http://www.techradar.com/us/news/internet/ibm-working-on-cloud-of-clouds-solution-to-limit-vendor-lock-in-1207375#null

[145] http://gcn.com/Articles/2013/05/31/Cloud-of-clouds-5-years-in-future.aspx?Page=3#

[146] http://internet-security-suite-review.toptenreviews.com/premium-security-suites/what-is-heuristic-antivirus-detection-.html
[147] http://www.welivesecurity.com/2010/12/29/what-are-heuristics/
[148] http://www.gfi.com/blog/defending-zeroday-threats/
[149] http://www.techopedia.com/definition/27451/zero-day-threat
[150] http://www.securitymanagement.com/article/zero-trust-model-007894
[151] http://www.securityweek.com/steps-implementing-zero-trust-network
[152] http://spyders.ca/reduce-risk-by-adopting-a-zero-trust-modelapproach-to-security/
[153] http://www.cymbel.com/zero-trust-recommendations/
[154] http://csrc.nist.gov/cyberframework/rfi_comments/040813_forrester_research.pdf
[155] https://go.forrester.com/research/
[156] https://www.csoonline.com/article/3250086/data-protection/7-cyber-security-trends-to-watch-out-for-in-2018.html
[157] https://gcn.com/articles/2018/01/05/ai-cybersecurity.aspx
[158] https://www.darkreading.com/threat-intelligence/ai-in-cybersecurity-where-we-stand-and-where-we-need-to-go/a/d-id/1330787?
[159] https://www.itproportal.com/features/cyber-security-ai-is-almost-here-but-where-does-that-leave-us-humans/
[160] https://www.linkedin.com/pulse/wake-up-call-iot-ahmed-banafa
[161] https://www.ibm.com/blogs/insights-on-business/government/convergence-blockchain-cybersecurity/
[162] https://www.forbes.com/sites/rogeraitken/2017/11/13/new-blockchain-platforms-emerge-to-fight-cybercrime-secure-the-future/#25bdc5468adc
[163] http://www.technologyrecord.com/Article/cybersecurity-via-blockchain-the-pros-and-cons-62035
[164] https://www.allerin.com/blog/blockchain-cybersecurity
[165] https://btcmanager.com/us-authorities-blockchain-covid-19-critical-services/?q=/us-authorities-blockchain-covid-19-critical-services/&
[166] https://www.govtech.com/products/Blockchain-Emerges-as-Useful-Tool-in-Fight-Against-Coronavirus.html
[167] https://www.expresscomputer.in/blockchain/could-blockchain-be-the-solution-for-surveillance-and-reporting-of-the-covid-19-pandemic/51670/
[168] https://www.ibm.com/blogs/blockchain/2020/03/mipasa-project-and-ibm-blockchain-team-on-open-data-platform-to-support-covid-19-response/
[169] https://mipasa.org/about/

[170] https://www.ledgerinsights.com/us-homeland-security-lists-blockchain-as-covid-19-critical-service/

[171] https://www.pymnts.com/blockchain/bitcoin/2020/bitcoin-daily-who-debuts-mipasa-blockchain-to-share-covid-19-data-coinbases-retail-payments-portal-passes-200m-transactions-processed/

[172] https://www.rollcall.com/2020/03/31/blockchain-could-transform-supply-chains-aid-in-covid-19-fight/

[173] https://www.blockchain-council.org/blockchain/how-blockchain-can-solve-major-challenges-of-covid-19-faced-by-healthcare-sectors/

[174] https://due.com/blog/a-new-era-of-crowdfunding-blockchain/

[175] https://www.disruptordaily.com/blockchain-use-cases-crowdfunding/

[176] https://blockgeeks.com/guides/Blockchain-and-supply-chain/

[177] https://www.forbes.com/sites/bernardmarr/2018/03/23/how-Blockchain-will-transform-the-supply-chain-and-logistics-industry/#c7c357e5fecd

[178] https://consensys.net/Blockchain-use-cases/supply-chain-management/

[179] https://www.technologyreview.com/2017/01/05/5880/a-secure-model-of-iot-with-blockchain/

[180] https://futureiot.tech/analysts-say-covid-19-pandemic-will-spur-iot-adoption/

[181] https://blog.infraspeak.com/iot-covid-19/

[182] https://www.bbvaopenmind.com/en/technology/digital-world/blockchain-technology-and-covid-19/

[183] https://davra.com/5g-internet-of-things/

[184] https://www.linkedin.com/pulse/iot-blockchain-challenges-risks-ahmed-banafa/

[185] https://www.linkedin.com/pulse/three-major-challenges-facing-iot-ahmed-banafa/

[186] https://appinventiv.com/blog/5g-and-iot-technology-use-cases/

[187] https://www.geospatialworld.net/blogs/how-5g-plays-important-role-in-internet-of-things/

[188] https://www.linkedin.com/pulse/iot-standardization-implementation-challenges-ahmed-banafa/

[189] https://www.linkedin.com/pulse/why-iot-needs-fog-computing-ahmed-banafa/

[190] https://www.linkedin.com/pulse/industrial-internet-things-iiot-challenges-benefits-ahmed-banafa/

[191] https://www.amazon.com/Secure-Smart-Internet-Things-IoT/dp/8770220301/

[192] http://www.computerworld.com/s/article/9245632/As_wearable_devices_hit_the_market_apps_are_sure_to_follow

[193] http://www.neongoldfish.com/blog/social-media/the-advantages-and-disadvantages-of-wearable-tech/#sthash.eij8N9WN.dpuf

[194] http://searchconsumerization.techtarget.com/opinion/Wearable-computing-devices-could-have-enterprise-prospects

[195] https://www.linkedin.com/pulse/20140424221437-246665791-affective-computing/

[196] https://www.linkedin.com/pulse/20140730042327-246665791-your-computer-will-feel-your-pain/

[197] https://explorerresearch.com/gsr-market-research/

[198] https://www.govtech.com/blogs/lohrmann-on-cybersecurity/chip-implants-the-next-big-privacy-debate.html

[199] https://www.npr.org/2018/10/22/658808705/thousands-of-swedes-are-inserting-microchips-under-their-skin

[200] https://www.cnn.com/2020/09/18/business/jobs-robots-microchips-cyborg/index.html

[201] https://www.thomasnet.com/insights/the-future-of-microchip-implants-in-humans/

[202] https://www.linkedin.com/pulse/three-major-challenges-facing-iot-ahmed-banafa/

[203] https://en.wikipedia.org/wiki/Microchip_implant_(human)

[204] https://www.linkedin.com/pulse/8-key-tech-trends-post-covid-19-world-ahmed-banafa/

[205] https://cointelegraph.com/news/new-tribes-of-the-metaverse-community-owned-economies

[206] https://biv.com/article/2021/11/top-business-applications-metaverse

[207] https://www.usatoday.com/story/tech/2021/11/10/metaverse-what-is-it-explained-facebook-microsoft-meta-vr/6337635001/

[208] http://www.cisco.com/web/about/ac79/innov/IoE.html

[209] http://internetofeverything.cisco.com/

[210] http://www.cisco.com/web/solutions/trends/iot/overview.html

[211] https://www.bbntimes.com/science/the-Metaverse-a-different-perspective

[212] https://www.mckinsey.com/industries/retail/our-insights/probing-reality-and-myth-in-the-Metaverse

[213] https://venturebeat.com/2022/03/24/5-common-Metaverse-misconceptions/

[214] https://www.mckinsey.com/industries/retail/our-insights/probing-reality-and-myth-in-the-Metaverse

[215] https://jarnoduursma.com/blog/7-misconceptions-about-the-Metaverse/

[216] https://analyticsindiamag.com/misconceptions-about-Metaverse-
      mark-zuckerberg-virtual-reality-augmented-real-world-gaming/
[217] https://www.weforum.org/agenda/2020/04/10-technology-trends-
      coronavirus-covid19-pandemic-robotics-telehealth/
[218] https://clearbridgemobile.com/five-emerging-mobile-trends-in-a-
      post-covid-19-world/
[219] https://www.sharpminds.com/news-entry/the-future-of-it-
      covid-19-reality-5-technology-trends/
[220] https://www.weforum.org/agenda/2020/05/why-covid-19-makes-a-
      compelling-case-for-wider-integration-of-blockchain/
[221] https://medium.com/datadriveninvestor/blockchain-technology-and-
      covid-19-c504fdc775ba
[222] https://www.zdnet.com/article/microsoft-cloud-services-demand-up-
      775-percent-prioritization-rules-in-place-due-to-covid-19/

Index

4G 177, 179, 212
5G 95, 177–182, 211–212

A
Adaptability challenges 148
Affective Computing 49–51, 62,
    189–192
AI 31–32, 34–35, 42, 45–47, 60,
    135–141, 143, 149, 176, 178,
    210–211
Apps 69, 74, 95, 176, 181, 185,
    199, 211
Artificial Intelligence 24, 31, 45,
    54, 149, 210
Authentication 22, 24, 75, 107, 110,
    153
Automotive 89, 180
Autonomic Computing 53–55

B
Bandwidth 83, 92, 94–95, 102, 106,
    178, 181, 212–213
Big Data 57, 59–62, 65–67, 69–73,
    75, 81–82, 89, 111, 115–117,
    151, 153–154, 195
Big Data Analytics 70, 115, 117,
    153–154
Bitcoin 22, 28, 30, 161
Blockchain 25, 27–29, 34,
    143–149, 155, 157–161, 163,
    165–169, 174–176, 181,
    213–215

Blockchain Literacy 148
Bluetooth 35

C
CDN 91–96
Chatbot 211
Cloud Computing 55, 79, 81, 84,
    101, 103, 105–107, 109, 111,
    113–117, 128, 131–133, 152,
    180, 208, 211
Complexity 22, 24, 66, 76, 102,
    148, 167, 177
Confidentiality 132, 146, 148
Connectivity 178, 180, 186, 212
Content Delivery Networks 91
COVID-19 24, 33, 59, 62, 157–161,
    173–176, 196, 209–215
Crisis Management 160, 214–215
Crowdfunding 163–166
CRQC 40–41
Cryptocurrency 22
Cryptographically Relevant
    Quantum Computers 41
Cryptography 9–11, 15–16, 23–24,
    28–30, 39–41, 145–146, 148, 169
Customer Trust 147
Cybersecurity 135–136, 138–141,
    143–145, 147–149, 195–196, 213

D
Dark Data 57, 65–67
Data Analysis 73, 154, 178

Data Center 82, 99, 106, 117, 144
Data Lake 73–77
Data quality 75, 146
Decentralized 72, 144, 148
Deep Learning 45–47
Digital Transformation 209
Distributed Ledger 146, 160

E
E-Commerce 91, 175, 180, 201,
 207
Edge Computing 81–84, 180, 213
Encryption 10–11, 15, 22–23,
 27–30, 75, 110, 133
Entanglement 6, 18, 28, 39–40

F
Fog Computing 1
Fraud security 146

G
gaming 204, 208
Gateways 13, 19, 84, 98

H
Hash function 28
Healthcare 14, 19, 21, 33, 89, 157,
 161, 175–176, 179, 181, 213
Heuristic Analysis 121, 125
High operation costs 148
Hubs 13, 19, 212
Human 18, 45–47, 49–51, 53–55,
 60, 62, 132, 136, 141, 169,
 189–191, 193, 195–196, 201,
 207, 209–211
Hyperledger 160

I
IIoT 181–182

Implementation 22, 136, 149, 153,
 174, 180, 182, 211, 213
Industrial 81, 89, 117, 179–182
Industrial Internet of Things 117,
 181
Infectious Disease 159, 214
Information Technology 45, 128,
 152
Integrity 54, 89, 107, 132, 146
Internet of Everything 55, 87–89,
 199
Internet of Things 84, 87–88, 111,
 115, 117, 139, 173, 177, 181,
 194, 199, 212
Internet Protocol 124, 137, 164, 212
Interoperability 110–111, 180, 204,
 206
IoE 55, 87–90, 199, 201
IoT 21–22, 24–25, 74, 84–85,
 87–90, 115, 139, 141, 169, 171,
 173–182, 194–196, 201, 212–213
IoT Security 139
IP 124, 137, 164, 212
Irreversibility 146–147
IT infrastructure 140

L
Latency 81–84, 92, 95, 177, 179,
 213
Logical Qubits 38–41

M
Medical Supply Chains 160,
 214–215
Metaverse 81–82, 84, 191,
 199–201, 203–208
Microchip 193, 195–196
Mirai 139
Mobile Technology 183

Modeling 59, 149
monopoly 205

N
Network Functions
    Virtualization 97, 99
Network Security 129, 151–154
Neural Network 45–46
NFV 97–100
NISQ 40
Noisy Intermediate-Scale Quantum
    Computer 40

P
Pain 59–60, 159, 175, 189,
    191–192
Pandemics 157–158, 209
Patching 138
Peer-to-Peer Transmission
Physical Qubits 38–41
Post-Quantum 41
Privacy 76, 89, 106, 131, 161, 186,
    191–192, 194–196, 201, 203, 213
Protocols 41, 54, 87, 110, 136, 200,
    207

Q
Quantum-Resistant 41
Quantum Annealer 40
Quantum Communications 15, 23
Quantum Emulator/Simulator 40
Quantum Internet. 13–14, 19
Quantum Supremacy 18, 24, 28, 33

R
Ransomware 22, 24, 135, 139, 213
Resilience 84, 146, 173
Robotics 47, 89, 215

Routers 13, 19, 98, 180

S
Safety 51, 179–180, 186, 191–192,
    195, 203
Sandbox 125, 129, 139, 153
Scalability 75, 94, 117
SCM 167–169
SDN 97, 99–100, 117
Security 9, 11, 15, 22–23, 25, 29,
    41, 54, 75–76, 83, 89, 98,
    106–108, 110, 114, 117,
    119, 121–123, 125, 127–129,
    131–133, 135–141, 144,
    146–149, 151–154, 161, 169,
    179, 181, 186, 191–192,
    194–195, 201, 203
Sensors 21, 49, 81, 83, 87, 89, 111,
    174–175, 178–179, 181, 190,
    194, 200, 207
Small Data 57, 69–72
Smart contracts 145, 147, 160,
    165–166, 215
Smartphone 185, 195, 204
Software-Defined Networking
    97, 99
Standardization 107, 180, 182
state-sponsored attacks 140
Storage 65, 67, 70, 72–76, 81, 84,
    89, 93, 95, 98–99, 102–103, 105,
    109–110, 112, 117, 133, 147,
    180, 195, 213
Storage limits 147
Structured Data 60, 66
Superposition 6, 39–40
Supply Chain Management 14, 19,
    145, 160, 167–168, 215
Sustainability 146

T

Technology 5, 7, 10–11, 13–14,
    16, 18–19, 24–25, 29–31, 33, 37,
    40–42, 45, 53, 55, 62, 71, 74,
    78, 88–89, 92, 94–95, 100–101,
    103, 106–107, 110–111, 113,
    115–116, 128, 133, 139, 141,
    144–148, 152, 157, 159–160,
    165, 167–169, 173, 176, 181,
    183, 191, 193–197, 200, 203,
    205–207, 209, 211–213, 215
Telemedicine 175, 181, 213
Teleportation 17–19
Thick Data 57, 59–62
Tracking and tracing. 160, 215

U

Universal Quantum
    Computers 40–41
Unstructured Data 60, 69, 76

V

Verification 24, 132, 145, 160,
    214–215

Virtualization 97–103, 107, 115,
    128, 152
virtual reality 61, 199, 201, 204,
    207
VR/AR 211
VUI 212

W

Wearable Technology 116
Web 3.0 84, 201
WFH 24, 95, 174, 211
WHO 10, 21, 30, 46, 60, 70, 74,
    76, 88, 92, 107, 111, 121, 132,
    141, 144, 158, 160–161, 164,
    166, 175, 192, 196, 199–200,
    207, 215
Wi-Fi 95, 123

Z

Zero-Day Exploit 122
Zero-Day Threat 122–123
Zero-Day Vulnerability 121
Zero Trust Model 127, 152–153
ZTM 152–153

About the Author

Ahmed Banafa, *Professor, Award Winning Author, Technology Expert and International Keynote Speaker*, has extensive experience in research, operations and management, with a focus on IoT, blockchain, cybersecurity and AI. He is the recipient of a Certificate of Honor from the City and County of San Francisco and the Author & Artist Award 2019 of San Jose State University. He was named as number 1 tech voice to follow, technology fortune teller and influencer by LinkedIn in 2018, his research has featured in Forbes, IEEE and MIT Technology Review, and he has been interviewed by ABC, CBS, NBC, CNN, BBC, NPR and Fox. He is a member of the MIT Technology Review Global Panel. He is the author of the book *Secure and Smart Internet of Things (IoT) using Blockchain and Artificial Intelligence (AI)* which won 3 awards, the San Jose State University Author and Artist Award, One of the Best Technology eBooks of all Time Award, and One of the Best AI Models Books of All Time Award. His second book was *Blockchain Technology and Applications* used at Stanford University and other prestigious schools in the USA. He studied Electrical Engineering at Lehigh University, Cybersecurity at Harvard University and Digital Transformation at Massachusetts Institute of Technology (MIT).